Ancient Civilization Mysteries

Written by Diane Sylvester ◆ Illustrated by Kathy Parks

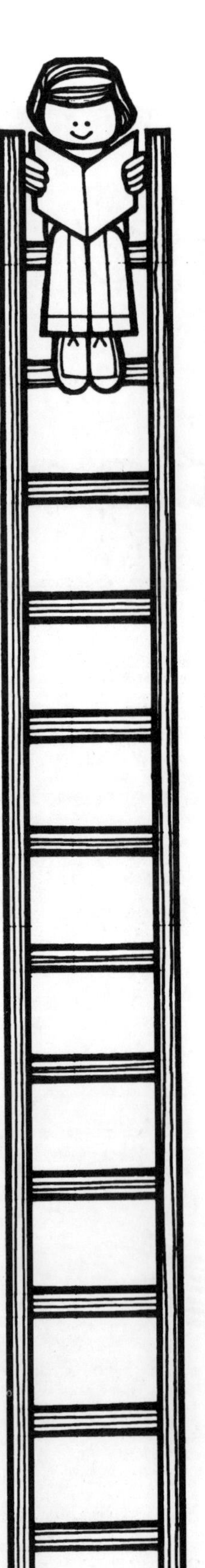

The Learning Works

Editorial production and page design by:
Kimberley A. Clark

LW 376

ISBN: 0-88160-307-4

Contents

To the Teacher 5–6

A World of Mysteries

The Fertile Crescent Puzzle 8–14

A River Runs Through It 15–18

The Mysterious Silk Road 19–22

Fib or Truth? 23–26

Ancient Religions Mix-Up 27–31

Clues to Ancient Writing 32–36

Architectural Wonders 37–40

Literary Scavenger Hunt 41–45

An Ancient Artifact 46–50

Invention Selection 51–54

Contents
(continued)

Mysteries in Special Places

Be Aware of Angry Gods! 56–59
(Ancient Greece)

The Mystery of the Stolen Shards 60–64
(Ancient Greece)

Search Along the Nile 65–70
(Ancient Egypt)

Let's Play *Q&A!* 71–75
(Ancient Rome)

Lost in Ancient Athens 76–79
(Ancient Greece)

Adventures in Mesoamerica 80–86
(Toltec, Olmec, Mayan, Aztec, Zapotec, Teotihuacan civilizations)

The Stolen Jade Necklace 87–92
(Ancient China)

A Tour of Kush and Axum 93–97
(Ancient Kush and Axum)

The Seven Wonders of the Ancient World 98–103

Glossary 104–105

Answer Key 106–112

To the Teacher

Purpose

Ancient Civilization Mysteries is designed to encourage students in grades 5 through 8 to discover more about the mystery and excitement of ancient peoples and cultures. By learning more about ancient civilizations, students will gain a greater understanding of the roots of all civilizations and an appreciation for the development of:

- languages
- the arts and literature
- government and democratic processes
- religious diversity
- scientific inventions and technologies
- economic concepts

Contents

The mysteries presented cover many disciplines including geography, the arts, literature, history, and architecture. Solving the mysteries and completing the activities are excellent ways for students to learn or improve their research skills using encyclopedias, the Internet, and other reference sources. These activities are also designed to sharpen students' map-reading skills through the use of atlases, globes, and world maps.

The first section, "A World of Mysteries," emphasizes topics that combine many ancient civilizations and includes subjects such as:

- the Fertile Crescent
- the world's great river systems
- great rulers of ancient times
- inventions
- writing systems
- architectural wonders

In the second section, "Mysteries in Special Places," students travel to some of the most important spots where ancient civilizations thrived, including:

- Greece
- Rome
- Mesoamerica
- Egypt
- Africa
- China

A glossary of terms appears on pages 104–105. Words used in the text which are set in bold italics are defined in the glossary.

To the Teacher

(continued)

Special Features

Each mystery in *Ancient Civilization Mysteries* is followed by two special features:

- **Discover More:** These are fun, creative, and challenging activities to supplement the theme of the mystery.
- **Learn More on the Internet:** Students can access the Web sites listed to find maps, pictures, audio selections, further reading, or additional activities that correlate to each of the mystery themes. (Although we are confident that all URLs we recommend are suitable for viewing by children, we cannot guarantee the quality or content of further related links on the WWW. Links on most of the sites have been checked, but some sites contain too many links to follow each to the end, and, of course, links change daily.)

How to Use This Book

Each of the mysteries in this book can be used as:

- **a whole-class activity** following a lesson or unit on a particular civilization. Call upon individual students to solve the clues. Have reference materials available, if necessary.
- **a learning-center activity**, where pairs of students or individuals work to solve the mystery. Include reference materials, picture books, and maps in the learning center.
- **a supplementary activity** to a unit of study on ancient civilizations.
- **an extra-credit or homework assignment**.
- **a cooperative learning activity**, where groups of students work together to complete the mystery.

A World of Mysteries

The Fertile Crescent Puzzle

Amazing architecture and mysterious artifacts! These words have caught the imagination of two friends who have met in Cairo to begin an adventure sponsored by Time Travel Tours. The trip will take them back in time on a tour of the Fertile Crescent, where the earliest known civilizations of the ancient world began.

The friends find a jeep with all the supplies necessary for a lengthy trip—but no tour guide. Then they see a note in the jeep which reads: "Unavoidable delay. Proceed as planned. Meet you in Jericho." They also find a briefcase containing a map of the Fertile Crescent, a notebook of drawings, and 10 description cards. The problem is that nothing is in order. Before the adventure begins, the friends must match the drawings to the descriptions.

First they realize that all the locations are identified on the Fertile Crescent Map. Now they need your help to match the drawings (on page 13) to the description cards. Can you identify the structures and objects depicted in the drawings and where they will be traveling to view them? (Note: Several of the locations are represented by more than one structure or object.)

Map of the Fertile Crescent

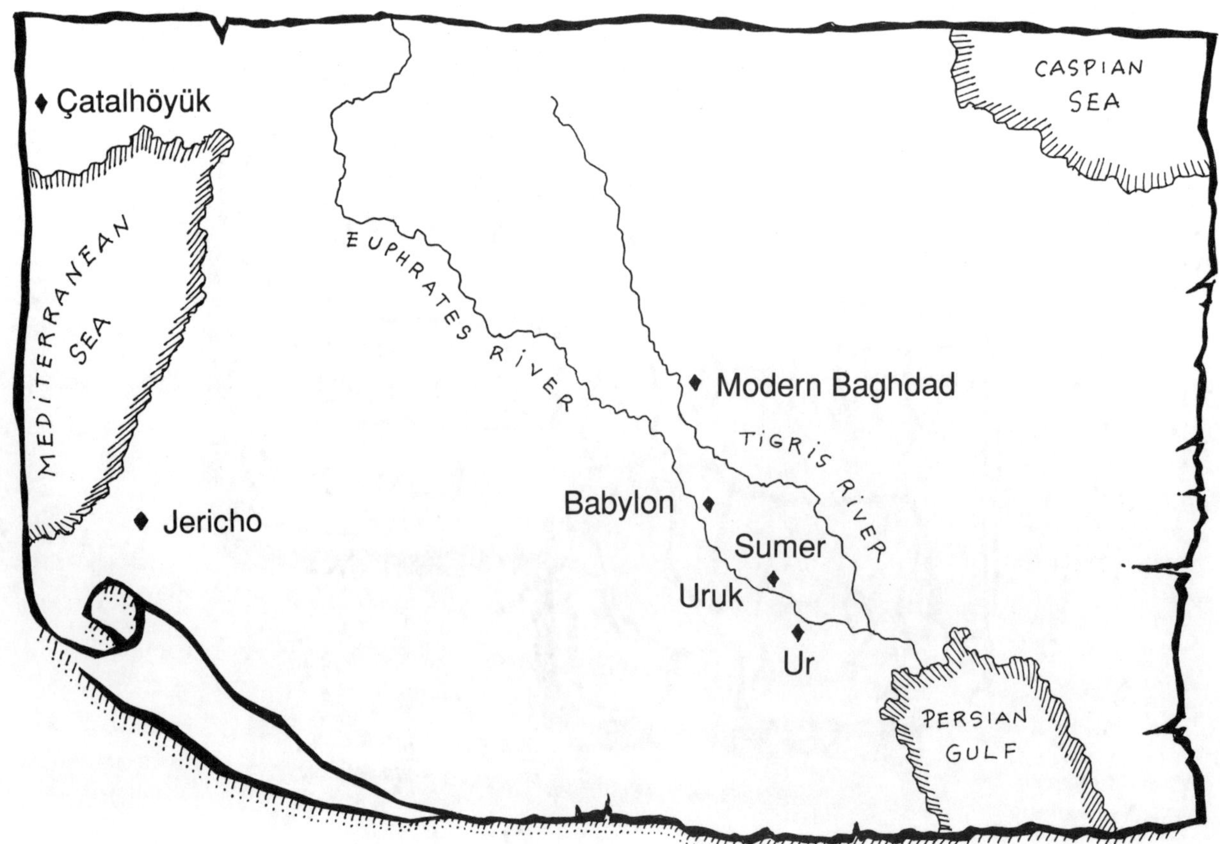

1. **Set time travel clock to 2100 B.C.** The visit here will astound you. You will see an amazing three-tiered structure which rises above the entire city. Murals and mosaics decorate the structure. Stairways on one side lead to the summit and to a shrine to the moon-god Nanna. The structure, built by King Ur-Nammu, is located in a major city of Sumer. According to the Bible, it was the early home of Abraham. **Present time:** It is approximately 187 miles (300 km) southeast of Baghdad, Iraq, near the town of Muqayyar.

   Identification of drawing: ______________________________

   Location: ______________________________

2. **Set time travel clock to 605–562 B.C.** As we walk along the main street of the largest city in the region, it isn't hard to notice this beautiful 23-foot (7-meter) tall structure. The terraced roof gardens were built by Nebuchadnezzar for his wife, who missed the hills of her own country. The terraces hold exotic plants and animals, waterfalls, and streams. **Present time:** All that remains of this city are mud brick foundations. It is about 55 miles (89 km) south of modern Baghdad, Iraq.

   Identification of drawing: ______________________________

   Location: ______________________________

3. **Set time travel clock to 6000–5000 B.C.** This is one of our more interesting stops. On the edge of the Fertile Crescent, this settlement is about 32 acres in size and has about 1,000 houses—interesting structures that are entered through doors in the roofs! Many of the buildings are shrines, as is the object pictured here—a stone statue of an animal that priests worship. The walls of the shrine are decorated with animals and human figures. **Present time:** The settlement is near Konya in modern Turkey; many artifacts found here can be seen at the Archaeological Museum in Ankara.

   Identification of drawing: ______________________________

   Location: ______________________________

4. **Set time travel clock to 3300 B.C.** Let's visit the place where a primitive form of writing began. This hollow object, made from clay found in the region, holds tokens which help people keep track of what and how much is being traded. Tokens are placed inside the object and while the clay is still wet, it is sealed. (If someone sends two baskets of grain to someone else, two tokens are put in the object. When the grain arrives, the receiving person breaks open the object and counts the tokens.) Ur and Uruk are two of the most important cities in this civilization. **Present time:** The region is located in what is now called Iraq.

   Identification of drawing: ______________________________

   Location: ______________________________

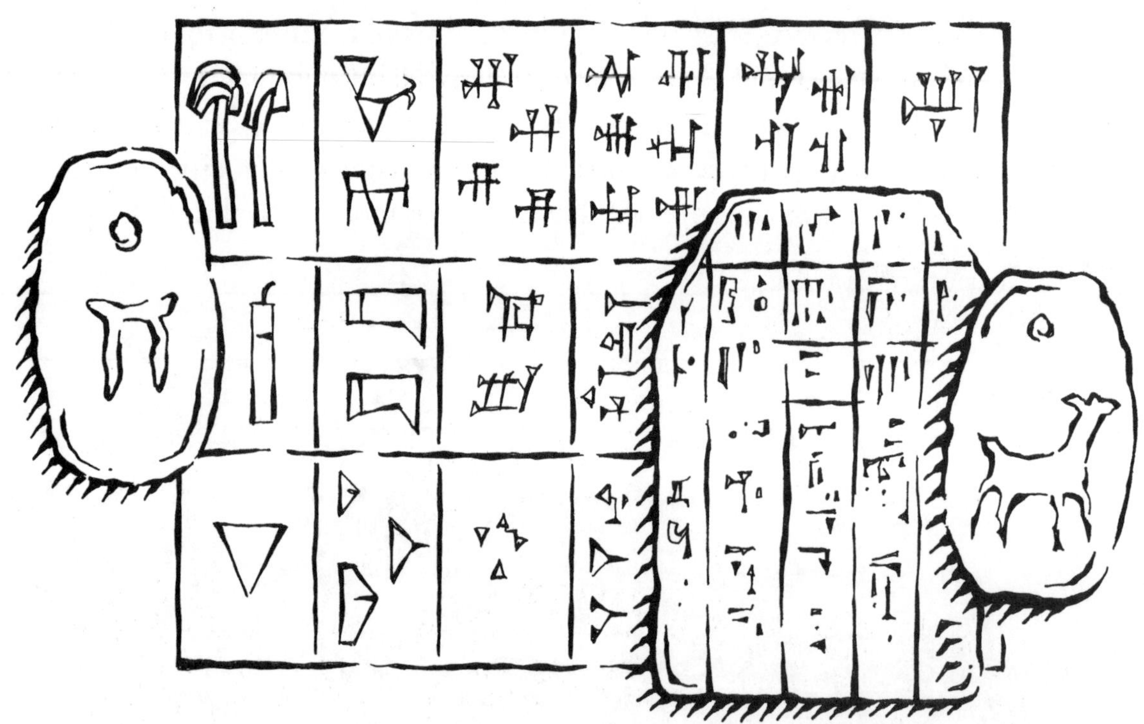

5. **Set time travel clock to 2500 B.C.** The people in this area use this type of seal to prove ownership. It is their way of signing their names, like we do today on documents. The seals are made by rolling carved stone cylinders over wet clay. No two seals are alike, so the owner can always be identified. On the seal are heraldic symbols, sacred emblems, mythological scenes, and a type of writing called *cuneiform* (which means wedge-shaped).

   Identification of drawing: ______________________________

   Location: ______________________________

6. **Set time travel clock to 612–539 B.C.** You will begin your walk through this city at this beautiful spot named for the goddess of love and war. It is one of eight such fortified spots leading into the center of town. It is decorated with glazed bricks inset with bulls and dragons. Nebuchadnezzar has renovated this city and made it more beautiful and more secure. After capturing Jerusalem, he forced thousands of its people to live here in exile. **Present time:** You can see this structure in the Berlin Museum.

   Identification of drawing: ________________________________

   Location: ____

7. **Set time travel clock to 1760 B.C.** The ruler of this dynasty established this code of laws for his people to follow. There are 282 laws in all. The main principles of the laws are that the strong should not injure the weak and that punishment should fit the crime. The laws also give some status to women and protect their property rights. The laws are carved onto *stelae* (stone slabs) and displayed in all the major cities of his kingdom. **Present time:** The best preserved stone stela of the laws was found at Susa, Iran, in 1901.

   Identification of drawing: ________________________________

   Location: ____

8. **Set time travel clock to 8000 B.C.** These items were used to build the early houses in this city—the oldest city excavated so far by archaeologists. They are made from mud or clay, shaped by hand, and baked in the sun. The citizens are well organized, and have built a stone wall to defend their city. The site is frequently mentioned in the Bible and is famous for the story of its capture by Joshua. **Present time:** The city is located by the Jordan River, 6 miles (10 km) north of the Dead Sea.

   Identification of drawing: ______________________________

   Location: ______________________________

9. **Set time travel clock to 2000 B.C.** This 3,500-line poem, about a king who lived around 2600 B.C., is one of the world's first epics. The epic is a myth because there is no historical evidence to support the tales of his exploits. Hundreds of years passed before it was finally written down on 12 cuneiform tablets. According to one part of the poem, the gods were angry and sent a great flood. They warned one good man, Utnapishtim, to build a boat. Everything was destroyed except Utnapishtim's boat, which came to rest on a mountain. **Present time:** The ancient Sumerian city ruled by this mythical king is called Erech in the Bible and is known today as Warka. It lies 156 miles (251 km) southeast of Baghdad, Iraq.

   Identification of drawing: ______________________________

   Location: ______________________________

10. **Set time travel clock to 3200 B.C.** This invention was probably first used for pottery making, but archaeologists have also found a clay tablet containing a pictograph of a cart using this invention that dates from the period 3200–3100 B.C. Most experts agree that this innovation originated in only one place and then spread to the rest of the world. **Present time:** This invention was first used in the area which stretches from the southern lands of Mesopotamia to the Persian Gulf.

    Identification of drawing: ______________________________

    Location: ______________________________

Amazing Architecture and Mysterious Artifacts

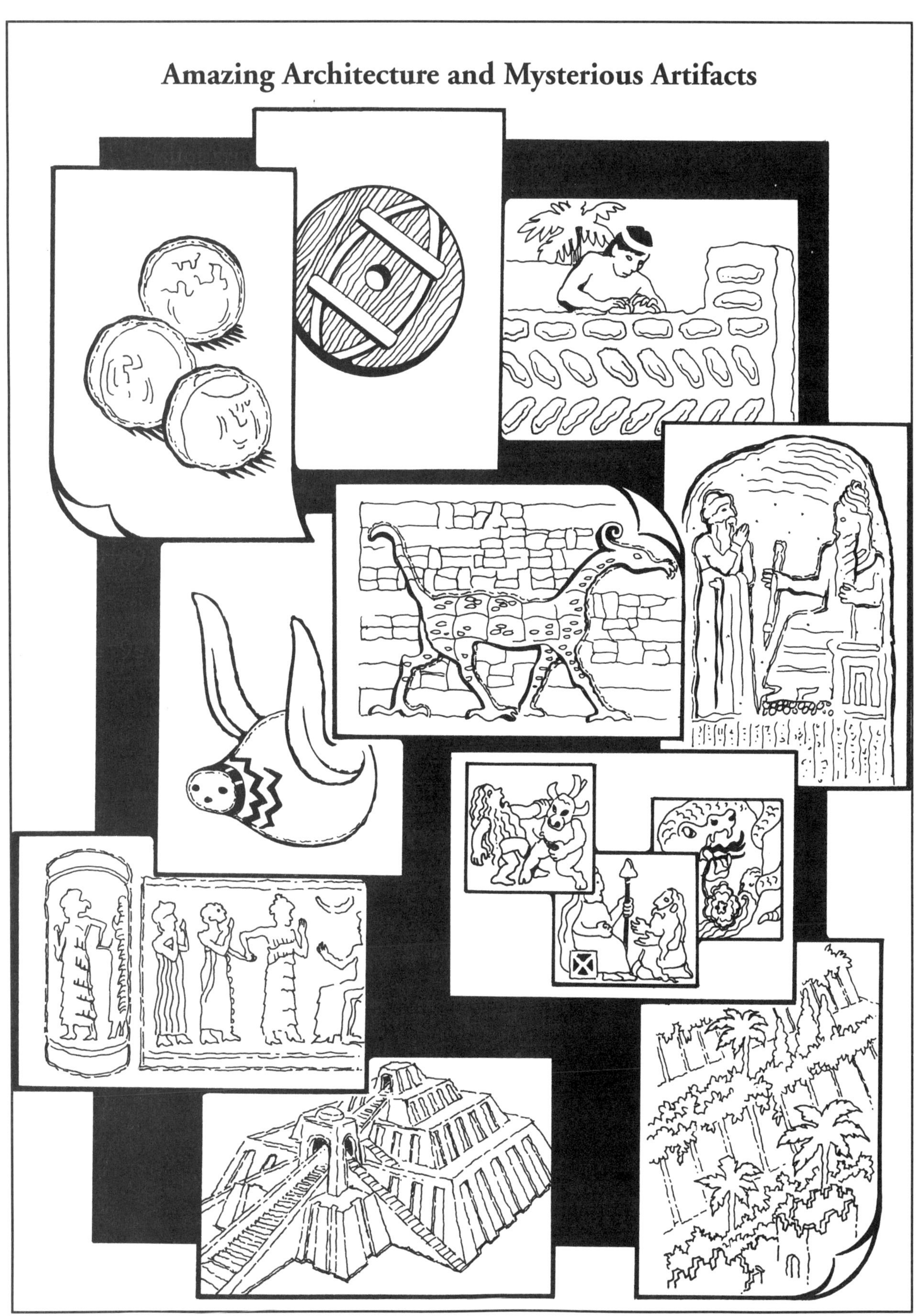

Discover More

- Make a list of the modern countries that are located within the Fertile Crescent zone. Find these modern countries on a map.

Learn More On the Internet

Çatalhöyük
http://catal.arch.cam.ac.uk/catal/catal.html

This Web site is designed for those interested in the ongoing excavations at Catalhöyük. Begin with Newsletter 4 and be sure to read the "winning essay competition."

Mesopotamia
http://www.garfield.k12.ut.us/PHS/History/World/meso/mesopotamia.html

The students who created this Web site have included information on Sumerians, Artisans, Phoenicians, and Conquerors.

A River Runs Through It

Amazing civilizations grew up along some of the major rivers of the world. Although the rivers often flooded and caused damage and death, the benefits of building a city or town along a river were many. For example, a river provided:

- a means of trading goods with neighbors
- a source of water to irrigate fields
- a means of transportation
- food in the form of water fowl, animals, and fish
- recreation
- an avenue for the exchange of ideas with people far away

You are about to take a trip back in time down some of the world's most famous rivers. The tour guides would like to show you a few of the towns that were located along these waterways and some of the people and animals that lived there. The tour guides are experts on geography and history, but they want you to figure out the names of these famous rivers of the ancient world.

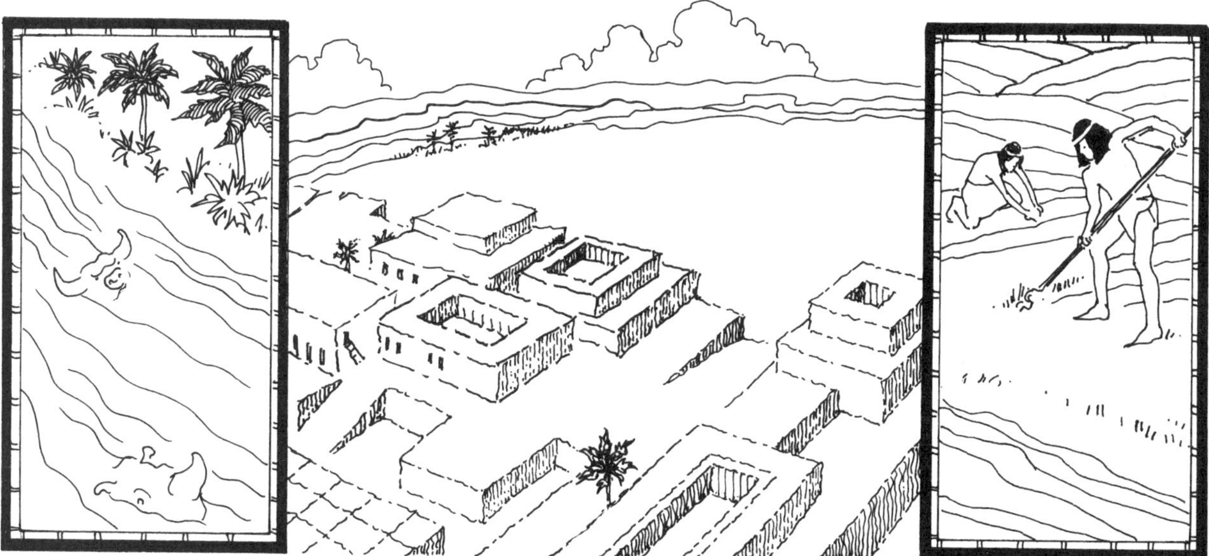

1. **2000 B.C.** We are sailing along a river fed by glaciers in the Himalayas. Eventually the waters of this river will reach the Indian Ocean. Look, over there—do you see the buffalo and rhinoceros bobbing in the water? Our small boat is now passing the large town of Mohenjo-Daro, home to 40,000 people. Those are farmers tending fields of barley, melons, and dates. The fields are irrigated by the waters of this river. The city is amazing for its time. It is laid out in a grid plan with a series of rectangular blocks of buildings separated by wide, unpaved streets and subdivided by narrow lanes. The houses are made of brick and most of them have their own bathrooms!

2. **670 B.C.** The source of the river we are on now is high in the mountains of Turkey. It is 1,180 miles long (1,900 km) and flows through the area called Mesopotamia (modern Iraq). It eventually empties into the Persian Gulf. This river supplies a rich soil perfect for growing barley, wheat, onions, and other fruits and vegetables. Ditches carry water from the river to the fields. Over there on the left bank you see the city of Nineveh, the capital of Assyria. The palace on the hill belongs to King Sennacherib. It has 80 beautifully decorated rooms and a library with cuneiform tablets on literature, religion, and the sciences. The city wall has 15 great gates, several of which are flanked by statues of huge bulls. King Sennacherib has also built canals to provide water to Nineveh and to its municipal gardens, which are home to many unusual plants and animals.

3. **580 B.C.** Today we are on the longest river in western Asia—1,700 miles (2,737 km) long. This river begins in the high mountains of Turkey, flows through Mesopotamia (modern Iraq), and empties into the Persian Gulf. The huge city wall to your left surrounds the magnificent city of Babylon. The boats you see belong to merchants and traders who are sailing from the Persian Gulf up the river and into the city. We are going to follow them because this river flows right through the middle of Babylon. We'll stop for a break at one of the quays so you can see King Nebuchadnezzar's city up close. Don't forget to walk past the famous Hanging Gardens and the temple ***ziggurat***.

4. **27 B.C.** This river starts in the western slopes of the Apennine Mountains. It is joined by other small streams as it flows 250 miles (402 km) southward and westward to the Mediterranean Sea. Rome, the city you are looking at now, was founded on the seven hills near the river. The people love the river because it offers water to irrigate their land, provides access to the sea, and protects them from invasion. We decided to visit this city at this time so you could see the inauguration of Octavian as the new emperor of Rome.

5. **7000 B.C.** We've gone way back in time so you could visit Jericho—one of the oldest towns located along this river. The river itself meanders from Mount Hermon to the Dead Sea, 296 feet (90 m) below sea level, where it empties. The river is unsuitable for navigation because it is so shallow, but the water it provides makes Jericho a good agricultural town.

6. **1338 B.C.** We are sailing along a river that is instrumental in sustaining one of the world's greatest civilizations. It flows from central Africa for 600 miles (966 km) to the Mediterranean. The river floods every July, and the floodwaters carry rich soil which is deposited over the fields. Notice the wild ducks, geese, and other birds. The river also supplies many fishes and animals for food. The smaller boats you see are made from papyrus stalks bundled together, but the funeral barge you see on the left is made of wood and is carrying the mummy of Tutankhamen to his burial tomb in the Valley of the Kings.

7. **500 B.C.** Like the rivers we have already visited, this is also called a "life-giving river" because the people's food supply depends on its waters. It is one of the most fertile of all agricultural regions, with rice being a primary crop. The river is also an important trade route. Its headwaters are in an ice cave on the southern slopes of the Himalayas. The river flows eastward for 1,557 miles (2,507 km) and eventually empties into the Bay of Bengal. We are passing the town of Kasi, one of the oldest existing towns in the world. (Later Kasi became known as Varanasi.)

8. **A.D. 200** This mighty river has it origins in the Plateau of Tibet. It twists through deep rocky gorges, makes a huge bend outside the Great Wall, heads southward, and flows into the Bo Hai, a gulf of the Yellow Sea. The region is known for its rich, yellow, windblown soil. Many people here consider it a river of sorrow because as many as a million people can lose their lives during a single flood. Nevertheless, as far back as 6000 B.C., people settled in the region. That's why it's called the cradle of this country's civilization. Since we are here during the Han Dynasty, we take our ***junk*** past Lanzhou (Luoyang), a major caravan center for the Silk Road.

9. **A.D. 610** We are sailing on the fourth longest river in the world. It is 3,400 miles (5,474 km) long and flows from the Kunlun Mountains in Tibet to the East China Sea. It is the main inland waterway and acts as an extension of sea routes. Floods are a problem along this river, too, but the soil is rich and agriculture thrives. We're taking you near the city of Hangzhou so you can see the Grand Canal, which was built by the emperor Yang Di. The Grand Canal links the two major rivers of China and is used to transport soldiers and trade items such as rice to northern China.

10. **A.D. 700** The river we are navigating now originates in Guatemala and flows northwest 450 miles (720 km) to the Bay of Campeche. It is one of the main trade routes for Mayan traders between Tikal and Palenque. We will take a short tour of Palenque and try to get an invitation to the royal palace. It has been rumored that if you are in the three-storied tower on top of the palace, you can spot visitors approaching along the river. You might see them carrying jade, quetzal feathers, jaguar pelts, salt, obsidian, or cacao beans. The Maya have a sophisticated system of trade.

Can you identify the rivers you visited? Write their names on the lines below.

1. ______________________	6. ______________________
2. ______________________	7. ______________________
3. ______________________	8. ______________________
4. ______________________	9. ______________________
5. ______________________	10. ______________________

Discover More

- Identify some of the more important American cities that are located along major rivers. Choose one of the cities and find out the problems and advantages this city has had in relation to the river.

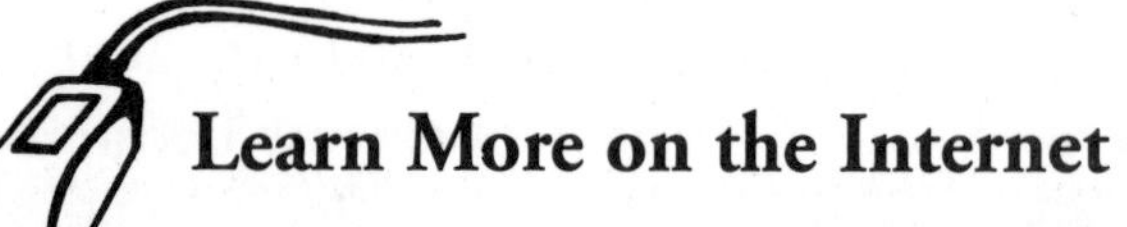

Learn More on the Internet

Rivers Seen from Space
http://www.athenapub.com/rivers1.htm

Rivers are perhaps the single most consistent natural feature associated with the location and discovery of archaeological sites. You can view major river systems from satellite and aerial views on this Web site.

The Victoria Nile
http://www.adventureonline.com/nile/learn.html

Learn about the African Nile and then click on Running the Nile for a kayak adventure.

The Mysterious Silk Road

The year is A.D. 800 and you are beginning a journey along the famous Silk Road, an ancient trade route stretching thousands of miles from the Mediterranean Sea to the capitals of China. You and the others in your caravan will travel the route to China, where you will trade linens, glass, and gems for silk, ceramics, and spices. Thousands of traders, pilgrims, soldiers, and adventurers have used this path before you, and thousands will follow you, including Marco Polo. The Silk Road is dangerous and difficult. You will be at the mercy of robbers, sickness, hunger, thirst, and the deadly desert heat. Each of the places below is a major stopping or crossing place along the Silk Road. Identify each place you stop as you proceed along the Silk Road to China.

1. You meet your companions in this city located between the Aegean and Black seas. As you wander around, you see bustling marketplaces, domed buildings, palaces, churches, and amazing mosaics, paintings, and architecture. You notice that the clothing worn by the wealthy citizens is made of silk. You learn that the Roman emperor Constantine rebuilt the city about A.D. 330, renamed it after himself, and made it the capital of the Eastern Roman Empire. Eventually, after more than a thousand years pass, this ancient trading center is renamed again and becomes Istanbul in the modern country of Turkey.

2. Your next stop is a great trading port located on the eastern shore of the Mediterranean Sea south of Sidon. You see all sorts of fascinating cargo being loaded onto ships bound for faraway places. This is an active commercial and manufacturing center and is famous for its woven silks, linens, and unique purple dyes. When it was part of Phoenicia, many carpenters and bronzesmiths came from this area to work for King David and King Solomon of ancient Israel. A thousand years from now this will be a small town, called Sur, located between Saida (Sidon) and Haifa, in the modern country of Lebanon.

3. You have many of the goods that will be making the trip to China, but now you will obtain linen from this city's famous weavers, who have developed their own distinctive patterns. The cloth is known as ***damask*** and it is a valued trade item even in China. You will also gather dried fruits from the surrounding gardens and orchards. This beautiful city is known as the world's oldest continually inhabited city and became the capital of Syria.

4. Your caravan competes for space with other caravans on the road as you head for the next city, which is considered the capital of the Islamic world. This great city is located near the Tigris River in what was once Mesopotamia. It is built in concentric circles with four gates facing toward the four points of the compass. Your caravan enters one of the gates and you follow the road until it comes to the center of town where you meet the roads from the other gates. Here are the bustling main marketplaces and the mosque and palaces. You stock up on supplies and trade for more goods. You don't know it now, but you are staying in the capital of the modern country of Iraq.

5. You have arrived at one of the many caravan cities along the Silk Road. Nomads live around here and caravans are exposed to raids, so you are anxious to reach the safety of its fortified walls. Formerly called Maracanda, this city is located in the Zeravshan River valley about 155 miles (250 km) north of the border of Afghanistan. Special quarters have been provided for caravans with shelters and areas for camels to rest and feed. It is said that this city has a population of over half a million people. In the future, its population will decrease as the Silk Road loses its importance, but it will remain an important city in Uzbekistan.

6. You've reached the foothills of the Tian Shan mountains and have come to an oasis irrigated by the Chirchik River. You will be staying in this Muslim city, which for centuries has been an important trading center. It is also one of the oldest cities in the world, as reflected by the meaning of its name: "stone village." In the twentieth century, it will become the capital of Uzbekistan.

7. Here you are facing some of the most forbidding mountains on your journey. Some of the mountains in this range are more than 25,000 feet (7,500 m) high. Some people call this region "The Trail of Bones" because so many men and animals die along the way. You may have to unload the pack animals and use human porters as you go across narrow passages. The descent on the eastern slope is the steepest and most difficult. This range of high mountains is located in the countries of Afghanistan, Tajikistan, and the Territory of Jammu and Kashmir. It is called a "knot" from which other great mountain ranges extend, such as the Tian Shan, Kunlun, Karakorum, and Hindu Kush.

8. You crossed the mountains safely. You now descend to the next trading city along the Silk Road. The view is spectacular! Glittering snowy ranges surround this town on three sides. This city marks the westernmost point of Chinese cultural and political influence. Many Chinese members of caravans end their westward journey here. Located on a fertile oasis in the Taklamakan desert, this town is famous for its variety of fruit. The town you are in is in the Chinese province of Xinjiang. The town's name begins with the letter "K" and ends with the letter "R."

9. You are about to cross the largest of China's deserts located in the Tarim Basin. It is a dreaded section of the Silk Road in the western part of the Xinjiang province. It is known as one of the driest spots on earth, worse than the nearby Lop Nor desert. You finally reach Dunhuang, an oasis town and the place where two Silk Road routes meet. It is famous for the Cave of the Thousand Buddhas.

10. After leaving Dunhuang, you press on toward your final destination. The caravan is about to end its journey after months of travel. You enter the arched western gate of this great walled city and make connections to trade your cargo. You will remain here for several months before making plans to get another caravan ready to go to the West. The city's name when you visit is Chang'an; today the city has another name. It is known for the 6,000 terra-cotta statues of warriors discovered in the tomb of the emperor Qin Shihuang. It is also the capital of Chaanxi province.

Can you identify the places you visited on your journey along the Silk Road? Write their names on the lines below.

1. ______________________ 6. ______________________

2. ______________________ 7. ______________________

3. ______________________ 8. ______________________

4. ______________________ 9. ______________________

5. ______________________ 10. ______________________

Discover More

- Learn how silk is made. Compare silk cloth to other natural fabrics like cotton and linen. Which fabric would you choose to make a shirt or blouse? Explain your choice.
- A famous legendary king, Schariar, ruled in Samarkand. His wife was Scheherazade. A classic work in world literature, *The Thousand and One Arabian Nights,* is a story about this king and queen, Ali Baba, Sinbad, and Aladdin. Check your library to see if you can find this piece of literature. Read the story and draw a picture of your favorite scene.

Learn More on the Internet

The Silk Road
http://www.xanet.edu.cn/xjtu/silk1/eng/silk.html

Follow the trail of the caravans and then click on Xi'an, Gansu, and Xinjiang to find out more about these important cities along the Silk Road.

Jewels of the Silk Road
http://phoenix.goucher.edu/~nmash/silk%20road.htm

This site offers in-depth information in the form of text and pictures on the cities along the Silk Road. Some of the information includes history, geography, and transportation.

Fib or Truth?

Using the magic of time travel, 10 of the ancient world's most famous people have agreed to appear on the television game show *Fib or Truth?*—and you are a contestant! The rules of the game are easy. All 10 people from the past will tell a little about themselves. You are to guess the identity of each person. There is an added obstacle, however. Two of the people are fibbing! They are only impersonating a famous person and don't have all of the facts correct. Can you spot these two? Good luck!

Participant 1: I am the greatest ruler of Babylon and have many visions for my people. I came to power in 1792 B.C. I have a strong army and have conquered all of Sumer and Akkad. Now I have brought prosperity and peace to the Babylonians. I am writing one of the most important codes of law ever devised. There are laws for protecting the family, personal property, and real estate. My laws give some status to women, and require that kidnappers and bandits be put to death. I am carving my laws onto stone monuments which will be displayed in all the major cities of my kingdom.

Participant 2: Hello! I bring greetings from Zoser, King of the united Egypt. I am an Egyptian priest, but my claim to fame is that I am an architect; in fact, some people call me the world's first architect. I designed the Step Pyramid at Saqqara and am now overseeing its construction. It is a series of six ***mastabas*** stacked on top of one another like steps. And it is the first Egyptian building constructed in stone! When Zoser dies he will be buried 80 feet (29 m) under the pyramid.

Participant 3: I, the Great Pharaoh of Egypt, greet you. I am a very powerful ruler and the son of King Snefru. This is an age of splendor in Egypt. I keep a grand court and people worship me as a god on Earth. I enjoy and support all of the arts, but right now I am focusing on the building of my pyramid. I have mobilized nearly all of the males to work on this monumental structure, for it is where I'll be buried when I die. The pyramid is located at Abu Simbel and is already being called the "Amazing Pyramid."

Participant 4: I extend a hand of friendship from India. I am India's first emperor and am called a military genius by my advisors. I think they are right because presently I have 9,000 war elephants and 8,000 chariots in my army. Commerce and industry are flourishing and artisans are prospering. An important part of my life is my religion, which is called Jainism. In fact, I am considering abdicating my throne, probably in 301 B.C., to enter a monastery.

Participant 5: Greetings to all from the kingdom of Israel. I am Israel's second king, and I worked hard to bring together all the tribes of Israel. I'm famous for the tactics I used to capture Jerusalem. Scouts were sent into the city through the water tunnel. Once inside, they opened the city gates and allowed the rest of my army to enter. I made Jerusalem the political and religious center for all my people. My son's name is Solomon, and I predict that he will be a great king, too.

Participant 6: I am the great uniter of all of China and its first emperor. Some people consider me cruel, but I prefer to think about all of the great things that I have done. One of the most important things was to standardize our written language. Now people who speak different languages can communicate with one another. I am also extending the Great Wall and completing a huge burial complex where my body will be placed when I die. One part of it has over 6,000 life-sized statues of warriors guarding my tomb.

Participant 7: Hello! You should know me because I am the brilliant general from Carthage in North Africa who crossed the Alps and defeated the Roman Army. Of course I had my brilliant army of 40,000 men and a force of war camels to help me win the battle.

Participant 8: I bring friendship from all the people of Greece. I am a philosopher, born in 427 B.C. I studied under the great Socrates and one of my pupils is Aristotle. I enjoy thinking creatively and talking about politics and logic. I started the Academy in Athens (thought to be the forerunner of your colleges and universities), an institution devoted to research and instruction in philosophy and the sciences. One of the dialogues for which I am famous is *The Republic,* in which I talk about the ideal state.

Participant 9: In Rome, people stand up and hail me. I'm the first Roman emperor and a skillful general. I conquered many lands for the Holy Roman Empire. I am also a clever politician and writer. I am personally responsible for reforming the Roman calendar, which came to be called the Julian Calendar. The Ides of March is approaching, and I have an important meeting that day, so I must hurry home.

Participant 10: "What you do not want done to yourself, do not do to others." Greetings from China. This is one of the sayings that I often use to teach people moral principles. I was born in 531 B.C. I spent many years as a wandering scholar and teacher. People call me China's first professional educator. It is rumored that I started one of the world's great religions, but I consider it more a philosophy or code of behavior.

Can you identify the famous people? Write their names on the lines below.

1. ______________________ 6. ______________________

2. ______________________ 7. ______________________

3. ______________________ 8. ______________________

4. ______________________ 9. ______________________

5. ______________________ 10. ______________________

Which two participants were fibbing? What were the facts that they got wrong? Write your answers on the lines below.

11. ____ : ____

12. ____ : ____

Discover More

- In your opinion, what qualities make a successful ruler or leader? What leadership qualities do you possess? Write a paragraph explaining whether or not you would like to be a leader.
- Who are some of the great leaders in American history? Choose one of them and prepare a short oral report explaining how this person shows leadership qualities.
- If you could be famous for one thing, what would it be?

Learn More on the Internet

The Ancient World on Television
http://web.idirect.com/~atrium/fawotv.html

This Web site provides a weekly listing of television shows on ancient civilizations, rulers, history, and geography.

Ancient Religion Mix-Up

You are putting together a *Who's Who of Modern Religions.* You have explained to your research staff that some of the religions which evolved thousands of years ago are still being practiced today in many parts of the world, but others died with the collapse of their civilizations. You have directed your staff to research the world's religions and to come up with nominations for inclusion in the book. Unfortunately, one of the researchers wasn't very careful! That means that all of the "ancient" religions nominated below are considered main religions of the world today—except for one. Since you are a clever book publisher, you should be able to identify the major modern religions, and the one that is not!

Religion 1: This religion originated in ancient India. Although it does not have a main holy book, it does have many sacred writings, including the Vedas. The Vedas are scriptures in the form of hymns and poems and are the world's oldest religious writings. Also, there is not one single person on which this religion is based. Its followers worship many gods including Brahma, Vishnu, Shiva, and others. The people of this religion have great respect for all life, and many are vegetarians who worship the cow and hold it sacred. A few of their beliefs include the concepts of ***reincarnation*** and ***karma.***

Religion 2: This religion is thought to be the only ***indigenous*** religion in China. The founder of this religion is Lao Tzu, a wealthy prince who became disillusioned by court life and wandered throughout China. One of the main books of this religion is called *Tao Te Ching* (The Classic of the Way and Virtue). Life's goal for followers of this religion is to avoid the pursuit of wealth, power, or knowledge. By doing this, one can concentrate on life itself and promote inner peace and harmony with the environment. An assembly of gods who are administrators of the universe are worshipped.

Religion 3: This religion, the world's largest, is based on the life and teachings of Jesus Christ. It originated in ancient Israel. Followers of this religion worship one God, and believe that Jesus was sent by God to Earth. They believe that by embracing Jesus' ministry, death, and resurrection, they will achieve salvation. The main book of this religion is the Bible, which consists of the Old Testament and the New Testament. The teachings of Jesus are contained in the Gospels, the first four books of the New Testament. This religion is divided into hundreds of denominations including the Roman Catholic, the Eastern Orthodox, and the Protestant churches. Each denomination has unique doctrines and practices.

Religion 4: Of the three main religions in the world, this one is the oldest. It originated in ancient Israel. Followers of this religion believe in one God as creator and ruler of the universe. The founder of this faith was a nomadic herdsman named Abraham who was born in Ur in Mesopotamia. At God's command, he moved his people and flocks to Canaan. The "contract" between God and Abraham is called a covenant. The Torah (the first five books of the Old Testament) is a record of the history of these people, and contains customs and laws such as the Ten Commandments.

Religion 5: This religion got its start in ancient Turkey. The followers of this religion worship a mother goddess who controls the supply of food and the life and death of its believers. Religious services are held in shrines which are entered through doors in the roofs. The shrines are kept dark but are decorated with brightly painted plaster bulls' heads, life-sized leopards, scenes from daily life, and geometric patterns. During the harvest thanksgiving, people bring offerings of food to the altar and place them before statues of goddesses. This religion is known for its burial rites. A body is placed on a high platform and vultures are allowed to pick the skeleton clean. The skull and bones are then buried under a platform inside the family's house.

Religion 6: This religion is considered by many to be more of a philosophy than a religion. Its founder was born in China and became a wandering scholar who was given the title of Master K'ung. He is known as China's first professional educator. He taught that most of the ills of society happen because people forget their stations in life, and because rulers lose virtue and encourage warfare. He felt that social relations, proper conduct, and social harmony were very important. The books in this religion were written by Master K'ung and are known as the *Five Classics.* For nearly 2,000 years, they had to be memorized by people wanting to obtain government posts. Master K'ung is credited with this saying: "Do not do to others what you do not wish done to you."

Religion 7: This religion began in Mecca in what is now Saudi Arabia. It was here that Muhammad received the basic doctrine of this religion: There is no God but Allah, and Muhammad is the Prophet of Allah. This and other messages received by Muhammad were collected in the holy book, the Koran. In this religion, Muhammad is considered a prophet like Adam, Abraham, Moses, Elijah, and Jesus. The name of this religion means "submission to God," and its followers are called Muslims, meaning "those who have submitted." Devout followers of this religion pray five times daily, facing in the direction of Mecca.

Religion 8: This religion originated in Japan and its name means "the way of kami." Kami are superior powers and are believed to be the source of human life and existence. They reveal truth to people and give them guidance to live in accordance with it. An important figure in this religion is the Sun goddess, Amaterasu O-mikami, whose descendants unified Japan. There are no regular weekly services in this religion. Followers may visit shrines any time they want. This religion has no known founder. It doesn't have holy books like the Bible or Koran, but its two chief books are *Records of Ancient Matters* and *Chronicles of Japan.* They contain ancient oral traditions and deal with historical topics.

Religion 9: This philosophy and religion developed in ancient India. It was founded at about the same time as Buddhism by Mahavira, an ***ascetic*** saint. The goal of this religion is for the spirit of an individual to progress through a series of stages until it is able to conquer and renounce dependence on the world and the self. Followers believe in the equality of all souls and the principle of nonviolence toward all living things. Some believers do not eat meals at night for fear of unknowingly killing an insect. To free the soul, followers practice yoga, a discipline of self-control and meditation. They worship a large number of gods, goddesses, demons, and other divinities.

Religion 10: This religion was founded in India but entered China along the Silk Road and eventually gained more followers in China than in India. It was founded by Siddhartha Gautama, a prince who left court life and wandered as a monk. He taught that people should stop thinking only of themselves and their desires and possessions. They should practice the "Middle Way," a path that avoids extremes. Then a person can achieve *nirvana,* a state that frees a person from birth, death, and rebirth (*reincarnation*). Many images of the founder of this religion can be found in elaborate temples.

Identify the religions described, and write their names on the lines below. One line will be blank—that is the mystery religion that never made it into the modern world.

1. ______________________ 6. ______________________

2. ______________________ 7. ______________________

3. ______________________ 8. ______________________

4. ______________________ 9. ______________________

5. ______________________ 10. ______________________

Be an ancient civilization expert: Do research to identify the people who founded the ancient religion that never made it to the modern world. Write the name of the civilization on the line below.

11. ____

Discover More

- Learn more about the great religions of the world. Make a chart that compares their holy books, founders, main beliefs, and houses of worship.

- Each of the main religions has a symbol to represent it, such as the cross for Christianity and the Star of David for Judaism. Use reference materials to learn the symbols of five other religions. Imagine that all religions joined together for a day of peace and understanding. Create a symbol that illustrates this unification.

Learn More on the Internet

Try the following Web sites to learn more about the religions of the world and to help you gain a better understanding of the beliefs of others.

World Religions
http://www.snow.edu/~rogerb/wreligion.shtml

Rutgers University Virtual Religion Index
http://religion.rutgers.edu/links/vrindexb.html

Clues to Ancient Writing

As a sought-after private investigator, you are researching an important case at the Ancient Civilization Institute in Washington, D.C. While you are browsing through the stacks, a slip of paper falls out of one of the books. You examine it and realize immediately that it must be some kind of ancient language, and possibly an important secret code. You decide do some research on ancient writing systems.

First, you learn that writing systems have made possible technological advances that have taken people from simple existences of hunting and gathering to ones that included written myths and legends, great literature, science, and history—a permanent record of knowledge that could be passed on from one generation to the next.

Then you read that many language experts believe there were three great steps by which writing evolved from primitive ideography to a full alphabet. First came the use of signs to stand for word sounds; the Sumerians were the first to develop this stage of writing. The second was the creation by the Phoenicians of signs which became the prototype of all alphabets, and the third was the creation of the Greek alphabet, which included vowel signs.

Finally, you read about the ancient languages themselves. Now use the clues below to find out about early writing systems. Identify the name of each writing system and the ancient civilization in which each was created.

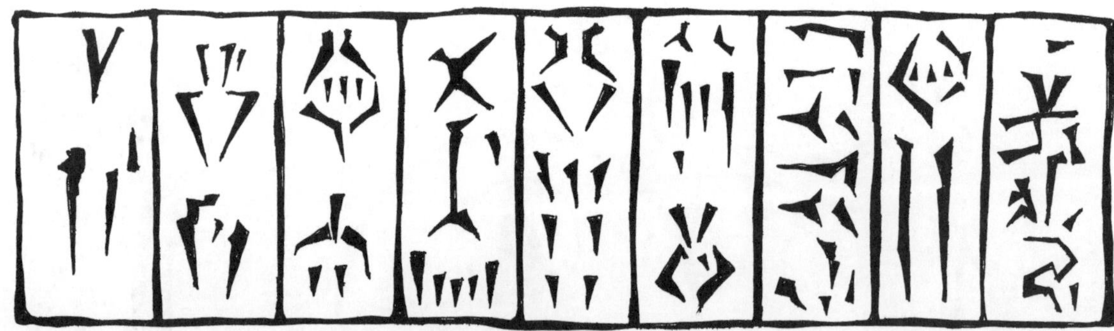

1. You start at the beginning of writing's history with the people who are the first known to develop a writing system. These people used clay found around rivers in their land in southern Mesopotamia to make tablets, and then pressed signs into the wet clay with a stylus that produced wedge-shaped marks. Each pattern stood for a sound or syllable. By adapting the signs and using them together, they could build words. This form of writing evolved from simpler pictographs which were transformed into a system of abstract symbols. One glance tells you that the message on the slip of paper is not written in this writing system.

2. Next you learn about a system of writing that was started along the Indus River by merchants who needed a method of record keeping. Carved out of soft stone, seals were used to make impressions in clay identifying personal property. Pictographs were carved on the seals along with interesting scenes of everyday life. They included pictures of animals, humans, and gods. About 250 pictographs have been identified so far, but scientists have not yet been able to translate the symbols, so it's a good thing your message doesn't match this kind of writing.

3. Experts on the Shang Dynasty have seen the emergence of writing on ancient bones or tortoise shells in this ancient civilization. The bones had a special name related to the fact that they were used to chart the future. The bones were heated and cracks appeared that were interpreted by the diviner as the seer's response to a query. Then the query, answer, and names of the people involved were inscribed on the bone. The writing that you have definitely does not look like these Chinese characters, so you quickly move on to another ancient writing system.

4. You discover that these people, originally known as Canaanites, were among the first people to use a system other than pictograms or hieroglyphs to make up words and concepts. They used 22 letters, all of which were consonants. This civilization was named from the Greek word *phoinix*, meaning "purple," which was the color of a dye they exported. Since your secret writing doesn't match the letters from this writing system, you pull another book from the shelf.

5. The book you're now looking at is about New World civilizations. These people had the only true writing system ever developed in the New World, which they probably learned from neighboring civilizations and adapted and expanded to fit their own needs. The language was based on the use of symbols, called ***glyphs***, which stand for numbers, names, and words. Over 800 glyphs have been interpreted. To thoroughly understand this writing system, a person needs to have an extensive knowledge of the civilization's mythology and folklore. You have to keep researching, because you don't have a match yet. By the way, this writing system has the same name as the Egyptian writing system.

6. This civilization developed an elaborate form of writing. At first the symbols were pictographs or small pictures of recognizable objects such as a man, a woman, a river, a sun, or a foot. Later, new signs were invented and the symbols came to represent sounds. Over 6,000 of these symbols have been documented. Other creative people of this civilization also invented a convenient material for writing made from the papyrus plant. Scribes were then able to use ink on papyrus paper rather than carving symbols into stone. Unfortunately, you don't have a match here, either.

7. The language of this island civilization was given a very scientific name by Sir Arthur Evans who, beginning in 1900, uncovered the forgotten civilization. He found some engraved personal seals with "squiggles" on them, which he believed were some kind of writing. Even after decades of study, though, Evans was unable to make sense of the writing, and it has never been deciphered. Consequently, little is known about the poetry and politics of these people. Language experts do know that, at first, scribes used pictographs, but in time they developed a ***linear*** script in which stylized symbols represented the sounds of the spoken language. The people of this civilization were named after their king, Minos. The squiggles of this language don't match your secret message, however.

8. Your research tells you that the writing system used by this ancient civilization was derived from the Etruscans. The language was rich in words necessary for intellectual discourse and had many military terms, which reflects the civilization's expertise in military operations. With only slight modifications, its alphabet has been adopted as the script of most modern European languages, including English. In fact, more than half of the words in English are derived from this language. The alphabet looks familiar, but it's not the one used in the secret message.

9. The people who lived in ancient Scandinavia used an alphabet consisting of 16 letters, or *runes*. The letters were made up of straight lines because they had to be carved on wood, metal, bone, or stone. These people erected engraved stones in memory of someone who had died or to mark their visits to distant places. Unfortunately, this is not a match either.

10. You've finally found it! The letters seem to match perfectly. Apparently the people of this civilization borrowed their writing system from the Phoenicians but they divided the consonants from the vowels and wrote each separately. There were 23 letters in this alphabet and the first two letters are called *alpha* and *beta*. One famous city of the civilization was Sparta. Many words in English have their roots in this language.

Can you identify the name of each of the writing systems and the ancient civilization where each originated? Write their names on the lines below. The alphabet or a sample of each of the systems appears beside the answer lines.

1. ______________________________

   ____

2. ______________________________

   ____

3. ______________________________

   ____

4. ______________________________

   ____

5. ______________________________

____

6. ______________________________

____

7. ______________________________

____

8. ______________________________

____

TENEME FV

9. ______________________________

____

10. ______________________________

____

Discover More

- Compare the alphabets of these languages: English, Russian, Greek, Latin, and Norwegian. List the letters that are different from the letters in the English alphabet. Other than English, which alphabet seems most familiar to you?
- Create your own alphabet of 20 letters. Use it as a secret code to write messages to your friends. Be sure to create a key so your messages can be translated.

Learn More on the Internet

Ancient Scripts of the World
http://alumni.EECS.Berkeley.EDU/~lorentz/Ancient_Scripts/

Find information and drawings of the symbols of ancient writing systems by searching "Index by Region" or "Index by Connections." To learn even more, click on "Resources & Destinations."

Architectural Wonders

Tanya and Emil are archaeological artists who make sketches of artifacts and buildings at dig sites. Their last assignment was to travel to hard-to-reach places to sketch the beautiful buildings and structures of the ancient world. They were at their final location and were packing up their drawings. They carefully paper-clipped a label to each drawing which explained the architectural structure and its location. They loaded their jeep, and were just about to drive through the jungle to the local airport, when a gusty wind came up. It howled and whirled and, in a second, picked up the portfolio and scattered its contents far and wide. When the winds died down, Tanya and Emil searched for the drawings but couldn't find them. Unknown to them, the drawings were found by the residents of a local village who realized they had found something important. They want to help out by replacing the labels before returning the drawings. Now they need your help to match the sketches on page 39 to the correct labels. Can you help them?

Labels for Architectural Drawings

A. Pagoda
   Description: *Buddhist tower temples have as many as 15 stories separated by overhanging, curled roofs.*
   Date: first seen around 2nd century A.D.
   Location: China

B. Temple
   Description: *The temple, rectangular in shape with carved columns supporting the roof, is a home for a god.*
   Date: 750–323 B.C.
   Location: Greece

C. Aqueduct
   Description: *Used to carry water great distances, some aqueducts are two or three tiers high.*
   Date: 753–476 B.C.
   Location: Rome

D. Hindu Temple
Description: *Religious in nature, Hindu temples are decorated with ornate, sculptured reliefs with no part of a wall left uncarved.*
Date: A.D. 320–750
Location: India

E. Mastaba
Description: *A flat-topped tomb with sloping sides, a mastaba has a pharaoh or nobleman buried in the ground beneath it.*
Date: The Old Kingdom
Location: Egypt

F. Pyramid
Description: *A temple rests on top of a 65-foot-high stepped pyramid that has stairs going up its four sides.*
Date: A.D. 650
Location: Mexico

G. Pyramid
Description: *A triangular-shaped stone structure made out of millions of blocks of solid limestone, a pyramid contains a pharaoh's burial chamber.*
Date: 2528 B.C. to the New Kingdom
Location: Egypt

H. Mosque
Description: *A domed, or vaulted, building, this Islamic place of worship sometimes has minarets. The domes were originally used as palaces.*
Date: begun around A.D. 684
Location: the Middle East

I. Stupa
Description: *The stupa is a solid dome used as a sanctuary for the remains, or relics, of the Buddha or other important individuals.*
Date: 2nd Century B.C.
Location: India

J. Ziggurat
Description: *A ziggurat is a huge temple tower made of sun-baked bricks with niches, murals, and mosaics decorating the structure. There are stairs leading to the temple on top.*
Date: 2100 B.C.
Location: Mesopotamia

Architectural Drawings of Ancient Structures

Place the letter of the correct description in the box on each drawing.

Mesopotamian Reed House

Discover More

1. You are a renowned architect. You are making a design for a new community center that incorporates the concepts of a pagoda, a pyramid, and a ziggurat into one building. Make your plans for the building on a large piece of paper. Explain your architectural concepts and how you see the building being used.

2. If you were to make a list of five modern buildings or structures that you think will be famous 200 years from now, which ones would you choose?

Learn More on the Internet

Archimedia I—Architecture in Ancient Near East
http://www-lib.haifa.ac.il/www/art/archimedia.html

This Web site allows students to understand what ancient buildings looked like and how they were constructed. A project of the University of Haifa Library, it focuses on buildings from Ancient Egypt and Mesopotamia.

Literary Scavenger Hunt

Myths and legends, religious books and traditions, and tragedies and comedies are just some of the literary finds from ancient civilizations. Put them together in a modern-day scavenger hunt and you have the ingredients for an intriguing puzzle. So if you're ready, let's begin! Oh, one more thing—you won't be told thc namc of the work of literature. From these descriptions, you will determine certain facts about each work. Use the lines provided to record your answers.

Item 1: Your search starts sometime around A.D. 750–800, when a group of monks from an island off Scotland started writing an *illuminated*, or decorated, manuscript of the four Gospels. It was completed at a monastery on another, larger island. It is written on thick vellum and lavishly illuminated with the rich ornamentation that was characteristic of the Celtic art of this period. There are fanciful figures and intricate designs of bands, knots, and spirals. This famous book is now housed in the library of Trinity College in Dublin.

Name of work: ______________________________

Country of origin: ______________________________

Item 2: One of the earliest books is this interesting work, which is written and illustrated on papyrus. It contains prayers, songs, hymns, and directions written in hieorglyphics, and was read during mummification and burial ceremonies. Murals show a priest dressed as the god Osiris reading from this book over the mummy of the deceased. This book consisted of scrolls which were funerary gifts buried with the deceased for use in the afterlife. The British Museum in London has one of the surviving books.

Name of work: ______________________________

Country of origin: ______________________________

Item 3: These manuscripts were found by a shepherd in caves in Wadi Qumran. They were written by a community of Jewish believers, called Essenes, who moved to the Qumran region around 150–111 B.C. The manuscripts contain religious literature, parts of the Old Testament, hymns, psalms, prayers, and biblical law. Some scrolls tell about life in the Qumran community. Approximately 500 scrolls, dating from about 250 B.C to A.D. 70, have been found and are currently being studied by an international community of scientists and theologians.

Name of work: ______________________________

Country of origin ______________________________

Item 4: This work is really five books which contain religious teachings and customs, laws, and history of an ancient people. They are traditionally credited to Moses, and although scholars recognize that the books contain real history, there is disagreement as to the accuracy of every action and word. In these books you can read about Moses leading the Hebrews out of slavery, the 10 plagues that God inflicted on Egypt, and Moses receiving the Ten Commandments. Every Jewish synagogue possesses at least one copy this work.

Name of work: ______________________________

Country of origin: ______________________________

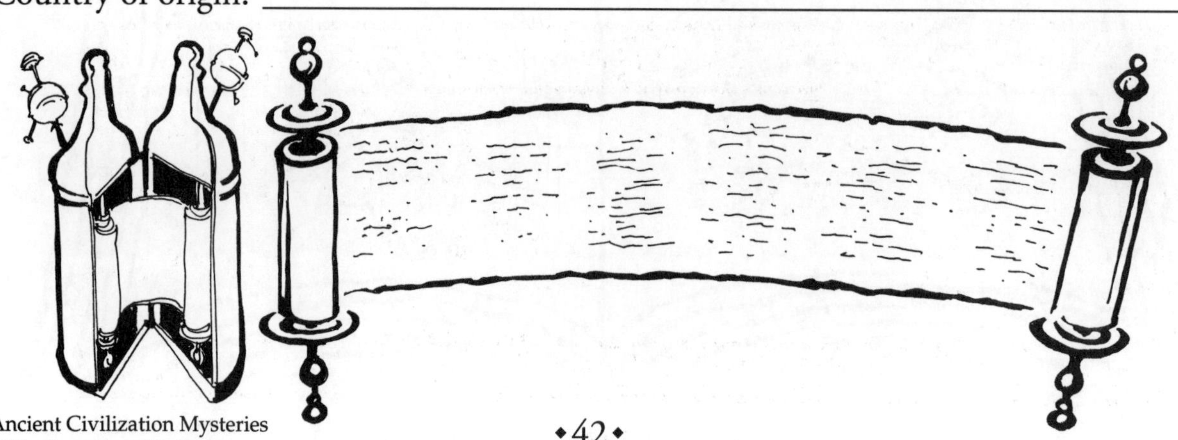

Item 5: This 3,500-line poem has been called one of the great creations of world literature. It was part of an oral tradition before it was written down on 12 cuneiform tablets sometime before 2000 B.C. The poem is about a warrior who is part god and part human. Scholars think there was a real ruler by the same name who was king of Uruk around 2700 B.C. The hero of the epic has many adventures. He goes into the wilderness to kill a giant, eliminates a divine bull sent to kill him, and dives to the bottom of the sea to find a plant which holds the secret to immortality.

Name of work: ______________________________

Country of origin: ______________________________

Item 6: You're now looking for the name of the most sacred books of Hinduism, passed on orally from one generation to the next by priests who memorized the texts and made sure no changes were introduced. Eventually, the texts were written down. They were developed by a people called the Aryans and date from between 1500–500 B.C. They are a collection of spiritual philosophies, hymns, and poems. Some of the gods mentioned in the work include Indra (god of thunder and war), Varuna (guardian of the cosmic order and moral law), and Agni (overseer of fire and light).

Name of work: ______________________________

Country of origin: ______________________________

Item 7: The man who created these stories was believed to have been a slave during the early 500s B.C. on the island of Samos. It is hard to separate historical fact from fiction regarding this author. He told his stories to illustrate a point or to teach a moral lesson by attributing actions and words to animals. Two of his well-known stories are "The Hare and the Tortoise" and "The Shepherd Boy and the Wolf."

Name of work and author: ______________________________

Country of origin: ______________________________

Item 8: You are now searching for an author born in 498 B.C. who produced numerous literary works. In fact, he wrote 123 plays and won 24 awards in annual dramatic contests. He is credited for introducing scene painting to the stage, enlarging the chorus (a group of actors who commented on the play's action and addressed the audience directly), and adding a third actor to allow for more complex scenes. One of his well-known plays is *Antigone.*

Name of author:____

Country of origin: ______________________________________

Item 9: Look for the author of *Tao Te Ching,* which is a collection of teachings. He is believed to be the founder of this country's only organized indigenous religion, Taoism. His teachings encourage people to return to a noncompetitive lifestyle and to live simply and in harmony with nature. He is quoted as saying, "A journey of a thousand miles must begin with a single step." The concepts of ***yin*** and ***yang*** are also part of his teachings.

Name of author:____

Country of origin: ______________________________________

Item 10: You're searching for the names of two works this time. They were first written down by Homer, a famous 9th century B.C. poet, but they originated as stories told in songs and ballads by wandering minstrels to Mycenean nobles. One work tells the story of King Agamemnon and other heroes who waged war against the city of Troy. The other work is an epic poem about a hero of the Trojan War. His journey home takes 10 years, during which the hero experiences many amazing adventures.

Names of works: ______________________________________

Country of origin: ______________________________________

Discover More

- Choose one of the literary works mentioned in this mystery and research it. Explain what it tells about the people of its time.
- Imagine that you have been asked to write a piece of great literature. What will you write about? Write a short paragraph explaining your choice.

Learn More on the Internet

Scrolls from the Dead Sea: The Ancient Library of Qumran and Modern Scholarship
http://sunsite.unc.edu/expo/deadsea.scrolls.exhibit/intro.html

This site contains information and pictures from the exhibition at the Library of Congress, Washington, D.C.

Mesopotamia—Gilgamesh
http://www.wsu.edu/~dee/MESO/GILG.HTM

This Web site provides background information, a series of questions to ask yourself as you read Gilgamesh, and an easy-to-read summary of the work—tablet by tablet. There are also links to other sites that provide more background information.

The Illustrated Encyclopedia of Greek Mythology
http://www.cultures.com/greek_resources/greek_encyclopedia/greek_encyclopedia_home.html

Access an A to Z listing of the characters and places in Greek mythology and read a detailed description of each.

An Ancient Artifact

The renowned archaeologist, Professor Anne Shunt, stood at the podium in the lecture hall. To her right was a secret object draped with a cloth. Professor Shunt told her class that while she was on a dig in the Middle East, she decided to wander through a nearby village. She went down a narrow side street and spotted an antique store. She entered the store, looked around for a few minutes, and was approached by the owner. He showed her the object and told her in a voice full of mystery: "I was given this ancient artifact many years ago. I think it was found in a tomb and ever since I've had it, I've had nothing but bad luck. Would you take it away and find the rightful owner?"

The students were anxious to see what was hidden under the cloth, but Professor Shunt said, "First you must guess the civilization it represents and then tell me where we must travel to return it to its rightful owners. Does anyone want to make the first guess?"

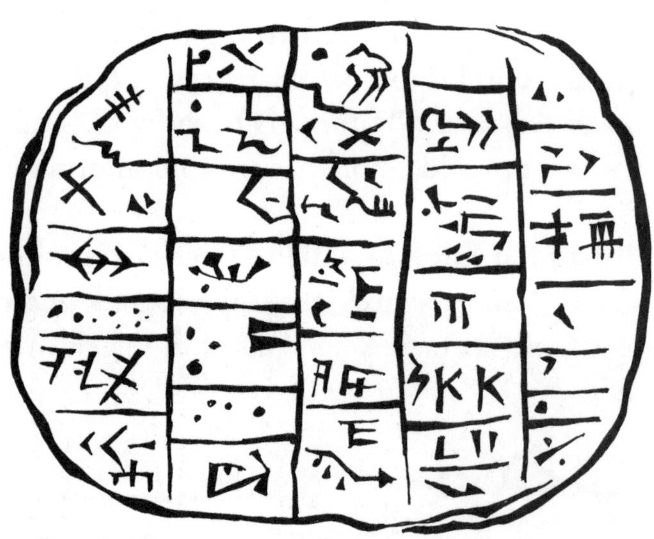

Student 1: "It must be from around 4000–2000 B.C., probably from southern Mesopotamia. I think it's a tablet with cuneiform writing on it, a form of writing developed by this civilization. They were an amazing people who invented the plow and the wheel, and used irrigation on a grand scale. They also built huge temple-towers called ziggurats."

"You've made an interesting guess," said Professor Shunt, "but this artifact is much bigger than a cuneiform tablet."

Student 2: "I'm guessing that it must be a stone with Hammurabi's Code of Laws engraved on it, probably dating from about 1792–1750 B.C. This civilization was located between the Tigris and Euphrates rivers. Nebuchadnezzar II (605–562 B.C.) was one of this civilization's most famous rulers. He captured Jerusalem and exiled thousands of Hebrews to his city where they were treated as slaves. Nebuchadnezzar built or improved many buildings in his capital including Ishtar Gate, the Hanging Gardens, and Etemenanki (also known as the Tower of Babel)."

"You certainly know your civilizations, but you've guessed incorrectly on the artifact. You're going to have to look west of the Tigris River."

Student 3: "How about looking northwest? If I am thinking of the correct place, the artifact is a shoe with an upturned, pointed toe, perfect for use in snowy mountain passes. The people who used these shoes lived in Anatolia and were fierce warriors. They are famous for a mechanical innovation: a battle chariot which gave them an advantage over neighboring armies. One of their kings hired a horseman to write detailed directions on clay tablets for the care and training of chariot horses. Their capital was Hattusa (Hattushash) and the name of this civilization begins with the letter 'H.'"

"That's an interesting guess about an interesting civilization," responded Professor Shunt, "but the object is bigger than a shoe."

Student 4: "I'm guessing it's an ivory carving with writing on the back. The civilization I'm thinking of is known for its ivory work. Of course, they invented glass blowing, so it could also be a piece of transparent glass. This civilization (1500–146 B.C.) set up trade routes with Africa, Egypt, Rome, Greece, and other places around the Mediterranean Sea. They were among the first people to use an alphabet rather than hieroglyphs. It consisted of 22 letters, all consonants. The three main cities in this civilization were Tyre, Sidon, and Byblos."

"How exciting it would be if the artifact were an ivory carving, but it's not. Are there any more guesses?"

Student 5: "Yes, I would like to try. I'm guessing that the artifact is a small fresco painting showing young men and women leaping over a bull. Bull-leaping was part of a religious ceremony for the people of this civilization (2500–1450 B.C.) and was a frequent theme on their famous fresco paintings. These people loved the sea because it gave them food, protection, and a means to trade. They also made beautiful pottery with complex geometric patterns. An interesting story about a labyrinth and a Minotaur takes place in their king's palace at Knossos."

"This is another interesting civilization, but you need to look farther west for the correct answer."

Student 6: "Could it possibly be the gold funerary mask believed to be worn by King Agamemnon? The civilization that produced this mask existed from 1650–1100 B.C., and its people were warriors, farmers, and traders. King Agamemnon probably raided a city called Troy in modern Turkey. One of the main cities of this civilization was Pylos, where the palace of King Nestor was built. Each palace in this kingdom had at least one cemetery, in which the rulers were buried in massive beehive-shaped tombs known as *tholoi.*"

"No, it's not the gold funerary mask," explained Professor Shunt. "If that had been taken, it would have made international headlines."

Student 7: "Well, I think I might know the answer. I believe it's a bronze urn with a funerary inscription on the bottom. The people who made the urn were the most advanced potters and metalworkers of their time (753–510 B.C.), although they borrowed many of their artistic styles from the Greeks. This civilization influenced the Romans who adopted their alphabet and religion, and used their engineering techniques in building roads, bridges, and arches. The Romans eventually assimilated these people and brought an end to their culture."

"All of you are making excellent guesses, but I want you to think about ancient civilizations that existed even farther west."

Student 8: "Okay, I'll take a stab at it. The artifact is a bronze brooch. It has a highly ornamental design pattern based on the circle. The metal has been intricately cut out. The people who made the brooch were experts at metalwork and enameling. Some of their designs included dragons or horses surrounded by plants. Their priests were called druids. Tribes of these people spread from many places in Europe all the way to the British Isles. They were defeated by the Romans in 225 B.C."

"The brooch sounds beautiful, but, unfortunately, that isn't the correct answer. So far all of you are thinking of civilizations in the old world. Now consider the new world."

Student 9: "That's a wonderful hint! I know what it is. It has to be a *quipu*, a device for calculating and recording numbers. It's made of colored and knotted cords attached to a base rope. The people who used the quipu lived in a country in South America and were expert engineers who built an extensive road system over the Andes. One of their sites is Machu Picchu, which has some of the world's finest stone structures. Their first settlements were started around A.D. 400, and they were conquered by the Spanish in 1533."

"You definitely went far enough west that time!" exclaimed Professor Shunt. "And you are very close. Now think about civilizations that are older than this one and located further north."

Student 10: "I know! It has to be the *codex* that the New World Archaeological Society reported missing. A codex is a type of book that, when opened, may be 20 feet (7.26 m) long. It was made out of tree bark which had been hammered into a type of paper, folded fan-shaped, and then bound between wood and animal hide. This civilization reached its height from about 300 B.C. to A.D. 600. The people used a hieroglyphic form of writing which scientists are beginning to decipher, and had a remarkable system of mathematics based on the number 20. They also used a sophisticated calendar system. Their huge ceremonial centers—such as Palenque, Copán, and Tikal—were a complex of temples, pyramids, plazas, ball courts, and palaces."

"Outstanding work! You guessed correctly. Now we must make arrangements to return the codex to the Society's museum."

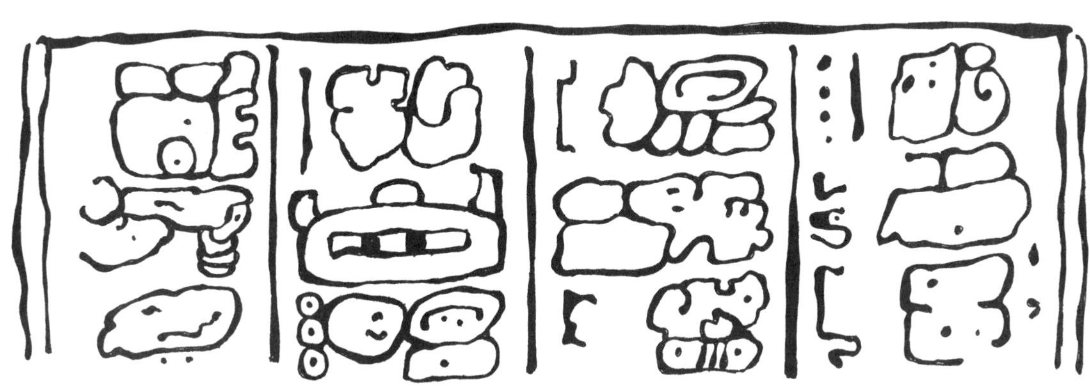

Identify the ancient civilizations and the modern places where they flourished. Write the civilization and the name of modern country or countries on the lines below.

1. ______________________________
   ____
2. ______________________________
   ____
3. ______________________________
   ____
4. ______________________________
   ____
5. ______________________________
   ____
6. ______________________________
   ____
7. ______________________________
   ____
8. ______________________________
   ____
9. ______________________________
   ____
10. ______________________________
    ____

Discover More

- Write a short story about the latest adventure you had while working with the New World Archaeological Society: locating a diamond-covered ceramic monkey which was taken from an emperor's tomb.

Learn More on the Internet

The Ancient Greek World

http://www.museum.upenn.edu/Greek_World/Intro.html

At this site you can view artifacts from the ancient Greek world at the Rodney S. Young Gallery of the University of Pennsylvania Museum of Archaeology and Anthropology.

Maya Adventure

http://www.sci.mus.mn.us/sln/ma/

View artifacts under "Maya Photo Archive." Then take a tour of "Maya Sites" and "Start Your Adventure!"

Invention Selection

Welcome to the International Museum of Amazing Inventions. We are going to select 12 world-changing inventions out of the hundreds here at the museum. Your tour guide will tell you about the invention, but will leave out the actual names of the inventions and the ancient civilizations where they were invented. Your challenge is to figure out both the invention and where it was invented.

As you take the tour, remember that our knowledge of which ancient people invented something first is based mainly on archaeological finds. Some great inventions may not have survived; others may not have been discovered yet. Also, some inventions may have started around the same time in different parts of the world. Now, let's begin our tour!

Use the Invention Selection Location Box on page 54 if you need help identifying the civilizations. Some of the civilizations in the box may be used twice. Dates below are ***circa***.

Invention 1. (c. 5000 B.C.) Farmers living in the southern region of the Tigris and Euphrates rivers discovered that certain plants could be cultivated and then kept alive by being watered. First they carried water in vessels. Then they diverted water from the rivers into their fields. Eventually, canals were made to carry water long distances from the rivers.

Invention 2. (c. 3200 B.C.) After papyrus paper was invented, scribes from this country needed something to write with. They extracted pigments of natural gum from the bark of the acacia tree and mixed them with soot. This invention probably made the pharaohs very happy.

Invention 3. (c. 3500 B.C.) Early farmers in cities such as Ur, Eridu, Kish, and Babylon broke up the ground with a simple digging stick or hoe. Eventually the hoe was weighted and handles were attached. Then this invention was pulled by an ox, which made tilling the fields much easier.

Invention 4. (c. 1800 B.C.) Surgeons from this ancient city-state invented items to help them perform simple medical procedures, such as opening abscesses. Hammurabi the Great probably had some used on him.

Invention 5. (c. 1700 B.C.) Several civilizations developed their own methods of writing, but this civilization produced the first true system for writing words. It contained 22 letters. This ancient civilization corresponds roughly to the coastal region of modern Lebanon.

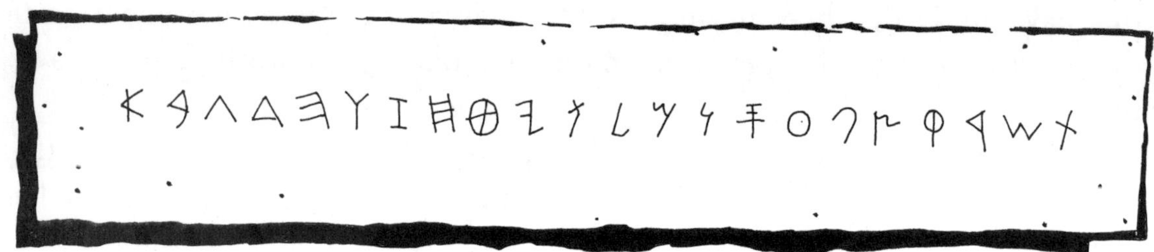

Invention 6. (c. 1200 B.C.) During the Shang Dynasty, bronze-casting technology developed. This meant that bronze could be cast and made into these devices, which produce a ringing sound when struck. The art of casting later disappeared and wasn't resumed until the 8th century B.C. The emperors of this ancient civilization used these devices in ceremonies.

Invention 7. (c. 690 B.C.) Where ancient irrigation canals passed over a valley, engineers built this device to bridge the valley. These were ambitious water systems. This civilization built one that had 30-foot-wide arches that carried a 60-foot-wide canal across a valley. The water was carried to the capital, Nineveh, to water the king's gardens.

Invention 8. (c. 537 B.C.) In the conquest of Babylon, Cyrus the Great led this civilization's army across the Euphrates River on a device supported by inflated animal skins. This is the earliest device of its kind on record.

Invention 9. (c. 236 B.C.) This simple mechanical device was used to lift water (and light grains of sand). It consisted of a tube bent into a spiral around a rod and was often used to direct water into an irrigation channel. Inventors in the land of the Pharaohs can claim this invention, but it was named after a Greek engineer who wrote about it in the 3rd century B.C.

Invention 10. (c. A.D. 105) A court official, Tsai Lun (Cai Lun), was probably responsible for this invention. He pounded together the bark of the mulberry tree, scraps of old linen, and old fishing nets. Then he boiled the mixture, pounded it again, and pressed it into sheets. The sheets were then dried and written on.

Invention 11. (c. A.D. 600) Although this invention is difficult to trace, its most likely inventors are the people from the land of the Ganges and Indus rivers who played a type of game called *chaturanga.* This is a game for two people played on a square board. Some of the playing pieces are called bishops, knights, and pawns.

Invention 12. (c. A.D. 950) The people of the Grand Canal and the Great Wall invented this ingredient for explosives. In the beginning, it consisted of large quantities of charcoal and burned fiercely instead of exploding. Eventually, it was refined and used for firearms and fireworks.

Can you identify each invention and the country where it was invented? Write their names on the lines below.

1. ______________________________
____

2. ______________________________
____

3. ______________________________
____

4. ______________________________
____

5. ______________________________
____

6. ______________________________
____

7. ______________________________
____

8. ______________________________
____

9. ______________________________
____

10. ______________________________
____

11. ______________________________
____

12. ______________________________
____

Invention Selection Location Box

China	Persia	India
Egypt	Assyria	Phoenicia
Babylon	Sumer	Mesopotamia

Discover More

- Create an invention of your own that combines a wheel, a plow, and a bell. Draw a picture of it and label the important parts. Explain what it does.
- Of the inventions mentioned in this mystery, which one do you consider to be the most important? Explain your answer.

Learn More on the Internet

Museum of Ancient Inventions
http://www.smith.edu/hsc/museum/ancient_inventions/hsclist.htm

The Smith College Program in the History of the Sciences highlights more than 20 fascinating inventions including a Sumerian Bull Lyre, a Cuneiform Cylinder Seal, Aztec Calendar Wheels, and a Chaldean Sundial.

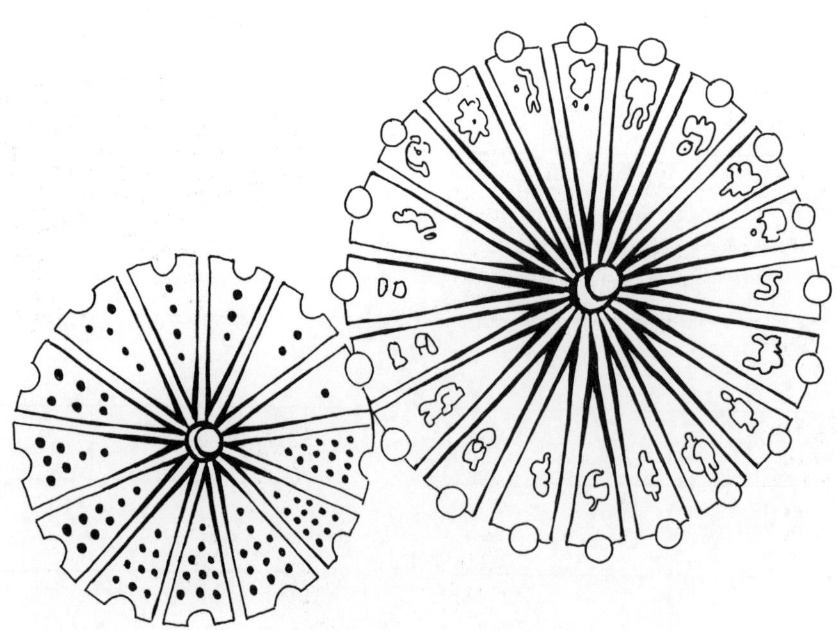

Mysteries in Special Places

Be Aware of Angry Gods!

Some young Athenian friends have decided to hold a costume party to honor the Olympians, the 12 gods and goddesses who live on Mount Olympus. The year is 450 B.C. They plan to meet at the Parthenon and parade through the ***agora*** to a shady spot under some olive trees. There they will eat the favorite food of the gods, ***ambrosia,*** and drink their special drink, nectar. Afterward, they will play games and tell stories. But our young Athenians may have a problem. There are 12 gods and goddesses but only 10 guests at the party. This means that two of the Olympians will be very angry because they will not be represented. Listen as each of the guests describes his or her costume, personal characteristics, and symbols. Can you identify the Olympians who will be represented and the two who have been left out?

Guest 1: "I will be representing the most powerful god on Mount Olympus, the king of all gods. I am ruler of the skies and can change the seasons. When I get angry I hurl thunderbolts at those who displease me, so I will carry a thunderbolt in my hand. I will wear a cape and a shield marked with an eagle."

Guest 2: "I will be dressed as the god of the seas, the second most powerful god on Mount Olympus. I also have a palace beneath the sea. It has been said that I am a difficult god and very greedy. If I am angered, I can generate tidal waves. I will be carrying a trident, a three-pronged spear, which can shake the earth. I will carry a wooden model of a chariot, representing my golden chariot which I drive over the seas."

Guest 3: "I am going as the goddess of the city, of handicrafts, and of war. My favorite city is Athens and my favorite bird is the owl. I will carry a poster with pictures of a ship, a plow, a flute, a bridle, a chariot, and a trumpet representing all the things that I invented. I will carry a magical shield which can turn my enemies into stone. I will also carry an olive branch."

Guest 4: "The god I'm going to represent is the god of music, archery, and healing. I will always speak the truth, for this god cannot lie. I will carry a lyre, a type of harp, and I'll play songs on it. I will sew pictures on my cloak of a crow and dolphin, my favorite bird and animal. If I really were this god, I would get to ride in my chariot every day and drive the sun across the sky."

Guest 5: "I get to be the goddess of love and beauty! I love birds and will make some models out of feathers to represent the dove, sparrow, and swan. I will carry a branch from the myrtle tree. I will wear a magic belt around my waist which will make men fall in love with me."

Guest 6: "I'm representing a despicable god—the god of war. Not even my parents like me! I will have to act angry and murderous, and try to make people fight with one another. I will wear a helmet with pictures of a vulture (my favorite bird) and a dog (my favorite animal)."

Guest 7: "I will be dressed like the queen of the gods with a golden crown on my head. I am admired by women since one of my responsibilities is to protect marriages. I will carry a large picture of my favorite bird, a peacock. I will wear a pendant of a tiny cow's head because that is my favorite animal."

Guest 8: "I am going as the god of fire and the forge. I will dress like a blacksmith because I make armor and weapons for the gods and goddesses. I will carry a hammer and tongs. Since I use volcanoes as my forge, I will pin a picture of an erupting volcano on my cloak. I am kind and peace-loving, so maybe I can help if Guest 6 gets out of hand."

Guest 9: "You're going to like me because I am sweet and gentle. I am the goddess of the hearth. Each city in Greece has a public hearth whose fire is never allowed to go out. Since my symbol is fire, I will design and wear a necklace that looks like flames. I will bring my little nephew with me to symbolize my love of home and family."

Guest 10: "I am going to wear a winged helmet and winged sandals to show that I am quick and clever. That is because I am the messenger for the king of the gods. I will carry a magic wand to guide me on my journeys. I am the god of travelers, of motion, and of sleep and dreams. I will carry a poster with pictures of a lyre, pipes, the musical scale, two men boxing, and stars to represent astronomy, because I invented these things."

Can you identify the 10 gods and goddesses who will be represented at the party?

1. ______________________ 6. ______________________

2. ______________________ 7. ______________________

3. ______________________ 8. ______________________

4. ______________________ 9. ______________________

5. ______________________ 10. ______________________

Identify the two Olympians who were left out:

11. ______________________ 12. ______________________

Discover More

- Pretend that you have been invited to the costume party. What god or goddess would you like to portray, and what would your costume be like? Make a drawing of the god or goddess in full costume.
- If the two gods who were left out find out about the party, what do you think they might do, keeping in mind their mythological characteristics? If you could intervene, what would you tell the two gods?
- Make two columns on a piece of paper. Label one column "Greek gods" and the other column "Roman gods." List the names of the Greek gods in the first column. Then translate each of the Greek gods' names into their Roman counterparts.
- If you decide to actually have a dinner party for the gods, you might want to serve food. Most supermarkets carry canned nectar in a variety of flavors. Ambrosia can be made by cutting up fresh fruits such as bananas, grapes, oranges, and berries, and serving them in a fancy bowl. You can also try this traditional recipe for ambrosia: Place together in a bowl several cans of fruit cocktail, several cans of mandarin oranges, and several handfuls of miniature marshmallows. Sprinkle with coconut (optional). Mix together with whipped cream or nondairy dessert topping.

Learn More on the Internet

Constellation List
http://einstein.stcloudstate.edu/Dome/clicks.constlist.html

At this site, you will learn about constellations and the myths upon which they are based. Constellations from the Northern and Southern Hemispheres are included, as are seasonal constellations. Click on a constellation to access information about the brighter stars of the constellation and the myths surrounding it.

The Olympian Gods
http://web.uvic.ca/grs/bowman/myth/gods.html

This site has excellent images of the Olympian Gods taken from works of art, coins, and other artifacts. Click on the word "Images" following the name of each Olympian.

The Mystery of the Stolen Shards

For years, archaeologist Deborah Blake wondered about the tale circulating at the dig sites in Greece about some missing broken pieces, or *shards*, of a valuable Greek *amphora.* (An amphora is a red and black vase painted with Greek figures and designs.)

One evening, as Deborah was organizing artifacts to be sent to a museum in Athens, she reached into one of the pots and made an amazing discovery. She pulled out a diary full of notes and drawings—some mentioning the missing shards! As Deborah read the diary, she realized it must have been written by the person who had stolen the shards. He had buried them and was going to reclaim them when he thought it was safe. But it wasn't going to be easy for her to find the shards, for the thief didn't hide all of them in one place. He had hidden one piece at each of 10 ancient Greek sites.

Below you will find the diary entries made at each of these sites. Next to the entry is a drawing of the missing piece. Help Deborah identify the sites where the shards are buried. Then cut out the shards and glue them together on a separate piece of paper so they form a drawing of the missing vase.

Shard A is hidden in the city located on the Saronic Gulf. This city is home to an acropolis which was rebuilt in the fifth century by Pericles. The shard is buried next to the Sanctuary of Zeus which is past the Statue of Athena and the Parthenon.

Shard B is hidden in the center of a famous plain located 26 miles (42 km) northeast of Athens. A type of modern foot race commemorates a battle which took place on this plain between the Greeks and Persians.

Shard C is hidden at the summit of the highest mountain in Greece, thought by the ancient Greeks to be the home of Zeus.

Shard D is hidden in the sparse ruins of this ancient city-state. A rival of Athens, this warrior state trained boys as young as seven for war. A term derived from the name of this city-state is used to describe conditions that are stark or designed to produce discipline.

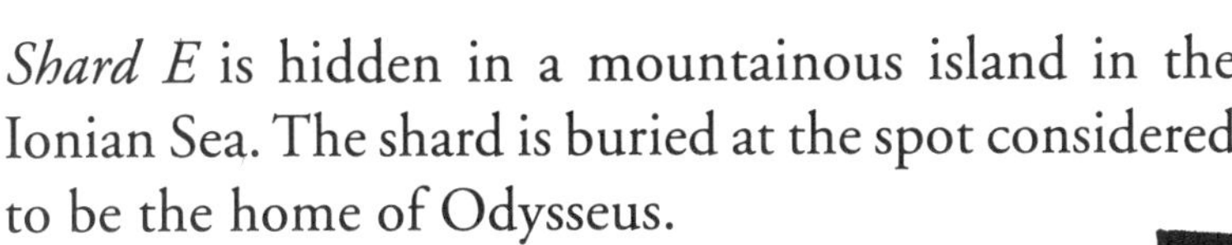

Shard E is hidden in a mountainous island in the Ionian Sea. The shard is buried at the spot considered to be the home of Odysseus.

Shard F is hidden in this sacred city of the ancient Greeks located on the lower southern slopes of Mount Parnassus near the Gulf of Corinth. It is buried near the temple within the sanctuary that was home to the famous oracle.

Shard G is hidden in this ancient Greek city in northeastern Peloponnesus near the ruins of a sanctuary to the goddess Hera. This city became the most powerful of the Greek city-states by the seventh century B.C., when King Pheidon defeated Sparta.

Shard H is hidden in the most important center of the Aegean civilization on the Greek mainland. Considered the capital of Agamemnon in the epics of Homer, it is situated on a hill dominating the Argive Plain and the pass to Corinth and fortified by great city walls. The shard is buried near the famous Lion Gate.

Shard I is hidden on the largest of the 200 Cyclades Islands in the Aegean Sea. Captured at different times by the Persians, Athenians, Venetians, Turks, and Russians, this island joined independent Greece in 1830.

Shard J is hidden in a small seaport located on an isthmus of the same name. It was a thriving commercial center and one of the great cities of ancient Greece. The shard is buried near the Diolkos, a paved causeway used to draw ships across the isthmus on rollers.

Can you identify the places where Deborah had to search for the missing shards? Write their names on the lines below.

A.	____________________	F.	____________________
B.	____________________	G.	____________________
C.	____________________	H.	____________________
D.	____________________	I.	____________________
E.	____________________	J.	____________________

Discover More

- Research one of the ancient Greek sites mentioned in this story. Write a report about the site and include sections on Amazing Myths, Cool Things to See, and Incredible History.

Learn More on the Internet

Pages Through the Ages: Ancient Greece
http://www.oakview.fcps.k12.va.us/~harris/96-97/agespages/greece/greece.html

This site on ancient Greece, with contributions by elementary students, has information on the alphabet, economy, government, religion, architecture, the arts, and conflict and war.

Greek Civilization Home Page
http://www-adm.pdx.edu/user/sinq/greekciv/carr.html

This Web site was designed by Portland State University sophomores for the use of middle school students investigating Greek civilization of the Classical period.

Search Along the Nile

The notorious Pyramid Pete, pilferer of antiquities, is on the loose again. During his latest caper, Pyramid Pete made off with a gold funerary mask from a museum in Cairo, Egypt. Fortunately for you—a world-renowned private investigator—Pete dropped a piece of paper that contained a list of ancient Egyptian sites. This may be the break you need! A witness said that Pete was heading toward the Nile River carrying the mask and appeared to be agitated and in a hurry. Your job is to investigate Pete's itinerary to determine the places he will visit, and try to head him off before he adds other artifacts to his cache.

Site 1: Check out the museums in this ancient and famous city founded by Alexander the Great in 331 B.C. Antony and Cleopatra lived here from 42 to 30 B.C.

You follow Pyramid Pete to ________ . You wish that you could do some sightseeing here. You remember that the Lighthouse, one of the Seven Wonders of the Ancient World, was located here. You rush to the Graeco-Roman Museum, but discover that you are too late. Pyramid Pete has made off with a crocodile mummy from the Egyptian Antiquities Room. The museum director said he spotted Pete running toward a boat docked on the Nile, and in the boat was a gold mask. Pyramid Pete slipped through your fingers this time, but you're sure to catch him at the next site. . . .

Site 2: Try to avoid the tourists at the Pyramids of Cheops (Khufu) and Chephren (Khafre) and hurry to the Cheops Papyrus Exhibition, a short distance from the Sphinx.

By the time you drive to ________ from the boat dock on the Nile, run past the Great Pyramid, and arrive at the Papyrus Exhibit, Pete has struck—he pilfered a valuable scroll of ancient papyrus that was on exhibit. You're tempted to take a tour of the maze of passageways inside the pyramid but you have nearly 12 miles (19 km) to go before you arrive at the next site that Pete might hit. Better hurry!

Site 3: Head for the region of many pyramids and mastabas. The most famous is the Step Pyramid designed by the famous architect and doctor, Imhotep, for the ruler Zoser.

When you arrive at ________ , you run immediately to the animal cemeteries where mummies of baboons, ibises, cats, crocodiles, and cows are buried. You're sure Pete will turn up here. But you're wrong; he's at the Mastaba of Ti looking at the mural reliefs, which are among the finest and best preserved in Egypt. He breaks off part of the mural showing peasant women making offerings. By the time you arrive, everyone is in an uproar. "Hurry," they urge, "he's heading for his boat. You might be able to catch him!"

Site 4: Located on the west bank of the Nile, close to the modern city of Cairo, this place was once the splendid capital of the Old Kingdom. It was founded by Menes, the first ruler of Ancient Egypt.

Pyramid Pete knows his ancient Egyptian history. You're sure that here at ________ he's headed to the Temple of Ptah, created to honor the god of craftsmen and artists. You see a figure running around a column and you yell, "Stop!" But you're too late. You notice that under Pete's arm is a statue of the god Ptah. On to the next site!

Site 5: This site was once the ancient city of Akhetaten, which was founded by Amenophis IV. The city is dedicated to Aten, the sun god. Contact Abi about hiring a donkey.

Your trip by donkey from the river to ________ , the modern name of the ancient city where Akhenaten built his Royal Palace, is annoyingly slow. As you bounce along, you think about Akhenaten, his wife Nefertiti, and his son-in-law Tutankhamen. You jump off the donkey as a man comes running toward you waving his arms. "The Aten jewelry is stolen! The robber is heading toward the river. You must pursue him!"

Site 6: Hire transportation to get to the ruins of this ancient city, located on the west bank of the Nile opposite the town of Qena at a wide bend in the river. A splendid temple dedicated to the cult of Hathor, goddess of love and joy, should offer many possibilities. (Hint: the name of this ancient city begins with the letter "D.")

The trail is getting hot now. You're sure that you'll have Pyramid Pete in custody soon. When you reach ________ , you rush to the Temple of Isis near the Temple of Hathor. You see Pete ahead darting in and out of the ruins. But alas, he escapes once more, causing great frustration among the guards at the site. They are sure that he has made off with a burial statue of Hathor, goddess of the sky, joy, and dancing. There is no time to lose now. You hurry to Site 7.

Site 7: A couple of miles northeast of Luxor, and close to the modern village with the same name, is this great temple complex. Within its boundaries are the Great Temple of Amun, the Temple of Khons, and the Festival Temple of Tuthmosis III.

You pass along the Avenue of Sphinxes, around the Sacred Lake next to the Great Temple of Amun, and into the temple ruins. Here at ________ , you're sure your search will come to an end. But our elusive thief has outsmarted you once more. The guard says there is a report of a missing scarab beetle amulet. There's no time to rest now. The scarab amulet is especially valuable, and you must catch Pyramid Pete before he leaves Egypt with his stolen treasures!

Site 8: Take the road to the nearby burial spot of many of ancient Egypt's kings of the 18th, 19th, and 20th Dynasties. This site is located within the Necropolis of Thebes. Search the area around the tombs of Tutankhamen and Ramses II.

Arriving at the ________ , you are directed by the tourist guide to the Tomb of Sethos I near the tombs of Tutankhamen and Ramses II. The guide believes she saw a suspicious person entering the tomb. You descend a flight of wooden steps and enter a long corridor with pillared chambers and numerous antechambers. The reliefs that line the walls of the tomb are excellent examples of ancient Egyptian art. You are sure to catch Pete now as you reach the end of the tomb where the King's sarcophagus and mummy were placed. But where is Pete? Could he have slipped out with that group of tourists that passed you in the corridor? This time he was extremely bold and snatched a box containing parts of a game, called *Senet*, which was popular with ancient pharaohs of Egypt.

Site 9: This town is now a market center, but it used to be the ancient Egyptian Tbot. According to ancient Egyptian religious folklore, this was the site where Horus fought a great battle with Seth. The Temple of Horus is the destination. An artifact will be left beside the colossal statue of Horus—the falcon wearing the double crown.

Even though you go directly to the Horus statue at ________ , you arrive moments too late. A witness says that a man snatched a ***canopic jar*** that had been placed by the side of Horus. The canopic jar must have come from an undiscovered tomb. This is very serious indeed! With only one clue left, you know time is running out. You have a boat ride and an airplane trip ahead of you—so hurry!

Site 10: You hire a pilot to fly from Aswan to this site of famous rock temples. The temples were constructed during the reign of Ramses II.

As you're flying from Aswan to ________ , you remember the rescue operation which saved the two temples from the rising waters of Lake Nasser when the Aswan High Dam was built. The temples were sawed into manageable blocks and reconstructed on higher ground. As the plane lands, you know that you will finally encounter Pyramid Pete face-to-face. You see him dash into the Hypostyle Hall of the Great Temple. You run into the Vestibule and back into the Sanctuary, and there he is—trapped! The tomb guard rushes forward to help you. Finally you have the notorious thief in custody. Egyptian law is strict regarding stolen antiquities, so you know that Pyramid Pete will be spending many years in prison. His expertise on ancient Egyptian history will not go to waste, however. He will be required to do research on new sites and to help restore damaged artifacts.

Fill in the names of the places you visited while following the trail of Pyramid Pete.

1. ______________________
2. ______________________
3. ______________________
4. ______________________
5. ______________________
6. ______________________
7. ______________________
8. ______________________
9. ______________________
10. ______________________

Discover More

- Which sites mentioned in the mystery would you like to visit? Learn more about one of the sites, and make a mini-poster that could be included in a travel brochure on Egypt.
- Identify the items the robber took, and draw a picture of each of them.
- The theft of antiquities is a serious matter, and international groups work together to stop plundering. Find out from local museum officials what steps they take to make sure they don't purchase stolen artifacts.

Learn More on the Internet

Splendors of Ancient Egypt
http://mfah.org/splendor/docs/highlts/

At this Web site, you can see images and descriptions of selected works from the Ancient Egyptian exhibit at the Museum of Fine Arts, Houston.

Egypt Fun Guild
http://www.seaworld.org/Egypt/egypt.html

This site is a Busch Gardens, Tampa Bay Educational Resource, and includes these sections: Hieroglyphics, Mummy Maze, Make Your Own Cartouche, Archaeologist's Challenge, Secrets of the Nile, Pyramid Power, and more.

Theban Mapping Project
http://www.kv5.com/html/home.html

Follow along with archaeologists at the excavation of KV5, which is believed to be the tomb of Ramses' sons. Click on Egyptology, Valley of the Kings, and Theban Necropolis for even more information.

Let's Play *Q&A!*

Welcome to *Q&A!*, the most challenging game show on television. As a contestant, you'll be given an opportunity to test your knowledge and win thousands of dollars! The rules are simple. Instead of answering questions, you will be given the *answers*. Your challenge is to come up with the questions. Each question that you guess correctly will be worth a certain amount of money. So remember, give your responses in the form of questions.

The category for tonight is "Ancient Rome." Let's play *Q&A!*

Answer 1: Worth $500

These twin boys are said to be descendants of the war god Mars. After they were born, a wicked uncle threw them into the Tiber River hoping they would die. A wolf saved them and a shepherd raised them as his sons. When they grew up, they founded the city of Rome.

Answer 2: Worth $700

This man was born in 100 B.C. He was a writer and orator, but is best known for being a brilliant general and an astute politician. He made numerous reforms including introducing the Julian calendar, enlarging the Senate, reducing debts, revising the tax structure, and extending Roman citizenship to non-Italians. He defeated all rivals to become dictator of Rome, and his likeness was portrayed on coins. Many people feared that he would make himself king, so they conspired to assassinate him. The conspirators killed him on March 15, 44 B.C.—the Ides of March.

Answer 3: Worth $400

This Roman emperor was Caesar's nephew and heir. He supported the leading writers and artists of his time, such as Virgil and Horace. He actually has two names, because a new title and name was conferred on this man in 27 B.C. by the Roman Senate. He carefully avoided the terms "king" and "dictator." He brought a time of peace and prosperity to Rome which became known as the Pax Romana or the "great Roman peace." He increased soldiers' pay and enlarged the Roman police force which reduced crime and public rioting. He died in A.D. 14.

Answer 4: Worth $500

These structures are complex architectural wonders. They were visited by men and women of all walks of life. These structures served a particular purpose, but were also sometimes used for exercising, playing games, or conversing with friends. Some important rooms in this structure include the ***thermae, frigidarium, caldarium,*** and ***tepidarium***.

Answer 5: Worth $200

Most of the government buildings and many temples in Roman towns were situated around this open area. It was patterned after the Greek agora. The one in Rome is considered the grandest in the ancient world. There were temples, a ***rostrum***, the ***comitium***, the ***curia, basilicas***, triumphal arches, columns, and statues. The road that ran through the center of this area was called the Via Sacra, or Sacred Way, the most famous street in ancient Rome.

Answer 6: Worth $800

The first of these three gods and goddesses of Roman mythology is considered the ruler of the universe, possessing the same powers as the Greek god Zeus. The religious center of Rome was his temple on the Capitoline Hill. The second is the goddess of the moon and hunting. She was the daughter of Jupiter. The third was the god of the sea. He could cause or prevent storms at sea.

Answer 7: Worth $600

This famous Roman was the first emperor to adopt Christianity. He moved the empire's capital from Rome to Byzantium, which he renamed Constantinople. He introduced many legal reforms in the years that he ruled.

Answer 8: Worth $500

This structure, with its arched vaults, corridors, and stairways, is an example of Roman engineering at its best. Nearly 60,000 people could come here to watch sporting events and to witness the killing and bloodshed of people and animals for amusement. Sometimes there were single combats, and sometimes there were mock wars staged between hundreds of fighters in one event. One time the arena was filled with water and sea battles were fought by gladiators in small ships.

Answer 9: Worth $1,000

This road was built by Appius Claudius and linked Rome with the Adriatic Sea. Many emperors repaired it, improved it, and built bridges and viaducts along it. There were also villas of the wealthy, funerary monuments, statues, altars, arches, and small temples on either side of this road. The Christian underground cemeteries along it are called the *catacombs.*

Answer 10: Worth $800

This prosperous Roman city was buried by an eruption of Mount Vesuvius in A.D. 79. More than 2,000 people perished as the city was covered under a layer of ash 20 feet (7.26 m) deep. It was rediscovered in 1748. Excavations have uncovered about 160 acres, or about half of the original city.

Can you give the questions for these answers? Write the questions on the lines below.

Question 1 ______________________________

Question 2 ______________________________

Question 3 ______________________________

Question 4 ______________________________

Question 5 ______________________________

Question 6 ______________________________

Question 7 ______________________________

Question 8 ______________________________

Question 9 ______________________________

Question 10 ______________________________

How much money did you win? ______________________________

Discover More

- If you could visit ancient Rome for one day, how would you spend your time? Who would you want to visit, what would you want to see, and what activities would you like to do? Record your answers in the form of a letter to a friend.
- Pretend that you are a journalist working for the *Pompeii Post*. You have to interview a prominent Roman for a feature article you are writing. Who would you interview and what questions would you ask the person?

Learn More on the Internet

Roman Republic Era
http://www.garfield.k12.ut.us/PHS/History/World/romanrepublic/romanrepublic.html

Ancient Rome
http://www.garfield.k12.ut.us/PHS/History/World/ancientrome/%7FAncientRome.html

The two sites listed above, produced by students and teachers at Panguitch High School, in Panguitch, Utah, are excellent sources of information on ancient Rome.

Daily Life, Ancient Rome
http://members.aol.com/Donnclass/Romelife.html

This site contains a wealth of information on ancient Rome under the categories of Breakfast, the Forum, School, Great Builders, Roman Families, Weddings, and more.

Lost in Ancient Athens

Sneecitophanes is at it again. The master thief of Athens has made off with a handsome painted amphora. The storage vessel he has taken is a highly-prized masterpiece fit for a nobleman's household. Painted red and black, it is decorated with images of plants, gods and goddesses, and animals. A witness saw him take it from the artist's pottery shop and hide it under his ***chiton***. That was easy because Sneecitophanes' chiton is bigger than most. He must have sewn in extra fabric at the shoulders to cover up his pilfered loot.

Let me introduce myself. I am known throughout the Greek empire as Secrates, detective extraordinaire. I have been investigating Sneecitophanes for months and this is my first break in the case. I'll be following him to see if he will lead me to the spot where he has hidden other stolen objects. Come along with me and identify the places Sneecitophanes leads us on the chase.

1. I follow Sneecitophanes to the center of Athens where I have to maneuver between stalls where fish, meat, vegetables, pottery, and animals are displayed. There are tradesmen everywhere. I edge my way around groups of men arguing politics and philosophy and groups of children playing hoops. I nearly lose Sneecitophanes as he ducks behind one of the ***colonnades*** surrounding the noisy and colorful square.

2. Sneecitophanes has slipped into this area where men and boys exercise and train for athletic competition. All around us men and boys are running, boxing, throwing the discus, and performing gymnastics. I almost bump into a group of philosophers discussing popular ideas with some of the young athletes. Luckily, I keep the thief in my sight.

3. I thought for sure Sneecitophanes would drop the amphora as he ran through the streets of Athens. I don't think he knows he's being followed, but he sure is in a hurry! He heads right into this large outdoor area (an important structure in every Greek town) and down the steep stairs where he stops in the orchestra to see if he is being followed. He might be suspicious; he nearly trips on a couple of masks near the ***skene***.

4. Sneecitophanes looks up. That means only one thing: he is heading for the road that leads from the town center below, to the hilltop above the town. I am used to seeing many people on this road, especially during religious celebrations. The biggest festival is held every four years to honor the goddess of our city, Athena, and a great parade winds up the road. But it is not a happy occasion this time. It is going to be a climb. Fortunately, I am in good condition and am able to partake of water at a fountain house just before the road gets steep.

5. The road leads to only one place, and Sneecitophanes knows exactly where he is going—to the top of the hill. The hilltop was once a fort for the defense of Athens, but now it is a holy place with beautiful white marble temples and breathtaking statues. Every Greek city has an area on a hilltop, but this one in Athens is thought by many to be the loveliest and most elaborate.

6. He enters through the only entrance at the top of the rocky hillside, at what is known as the entrance building. It is the gateway into the holy place. This beautiful structure was designed by the famous architect Mnesicles. He used ***Doric*** columns on the inner and outer colonnades, but inside he chose the more slender ***Ionic*** columns. Although never completed, a painting gallery and a sculpture gallery are located on either side of the central gate.

7. Once through the ceremonial gateway, he heads for a very small temple perched on a ledge to the right of the gateway. This might be where he plans to hide the amphora. This temple was built to honor Athena who brought victory to Athens. It is built of Ionic columns and was designed by Callicrates.

8. Sneecitophanes is definitely a sneaky character. He isn't in the temple for more than a minute when he hurries to the focal point of the hilltop complex of temples—a colossal gold and ivory statue of the goddess of our fair city, sculpted by Pheidias. From her vantage point she can see the whole city.

9. Sneecitophanes passes the statue and immediately veers to his right and enters the largest and most important temple in the complex dedicated to Athena. This temple is visible from the city below. The temple, Doric in design, is made entirely of white marble and surrounded by columns. It was designed by Ictinus and Callicrates, with sculptures by Pheidias. A ***frieze,*** depicting the Panathenaic Procession, decorates all four sides of the temple. I nearly forget what I am doing because the beauty of this temple is so overwhelming. But on with the chase!

10. Sneecitophanes is slowing down. Are we near the end of the trail? His shifty eyes scan the area before he sneaks behind a temple that has six *caryatids* (columns in the shape of female figures) supporting its roof. It is richly embellished and has rooms dedicated to Athena, Poseidon, and several local gods. The large porch on the north side protects a stone believed to have been struck by Poseidon's trident—at least that is the local story.

    Now I have him cornered and make my arrest. There behind the temple he had dug a pit which had carefully concealed more amphora, several ***hydrias,*** and a ***krater.*** The artists are going to be happy to get these pieces of art back, and to know that Sneecitophanes will be out of circulation for a long, long time.

Can you identify the places in ancient Athens suggested by the clues? Write their names on the lines below.

1. ____________________	6. ____________________
2. ____________________	7. ____________________
3. ____________________	8. ____________________
4. ____________________	9. ____________________
5. ____________________	10. ____________________

Discover More

- Find a picture of ancient Athens and the Acropolis. Trace the route that Sneecitophanes took while trying to hide the amphora. Choose a place not mentioned in the mystery that sounds intriguing to you and explain why you would want to visit there.
- Compare what life was like in Sparta with what life was like in Athens. Where would you have preferred to live? Explain your answer.

Learn More on the Internet

Architecture of Ancient Athens
http://harpy.uccs.edu/greek/athens.html

If you're curious to see some of the places along Sneecitophanes' route, access this Web site. There are pages of pictures of ancient sites in Athens as they appear today.

Daily Life in Ancient Greece
http://members.aol.com/Donnclass/Greeklife.html

Learn what it meant to be a citizen of Athens and other city-states. Find out more about family life, clothing, hairstyles, toys, pets, houses, and food.

Adventures in Mesoamerica

Traveling to exotic places is one of the highlights of being an intern for the Museum of Archaeology. Today, I'm off on another one of my adventures to find Dr. Audrey Gonzales, an archaeologist specializing in Mesoamerican civilizations. (Mesoamerican is a term used to describe the culture of the native peoples of central and southern Mexico, Guatemala, Belize, western Honduras, and El Salvador.) It's important that I find her so I can give her the latest translation of the Mayan glyphs from a stela which will help her in her work. Last I heard, she was working in a place where she uncovered a monument dedicated to a king named Pacal. Do you know at which Mesoamerican site she might be working? I hope so, because I need your help with my quest to find Dr. Gonzales.

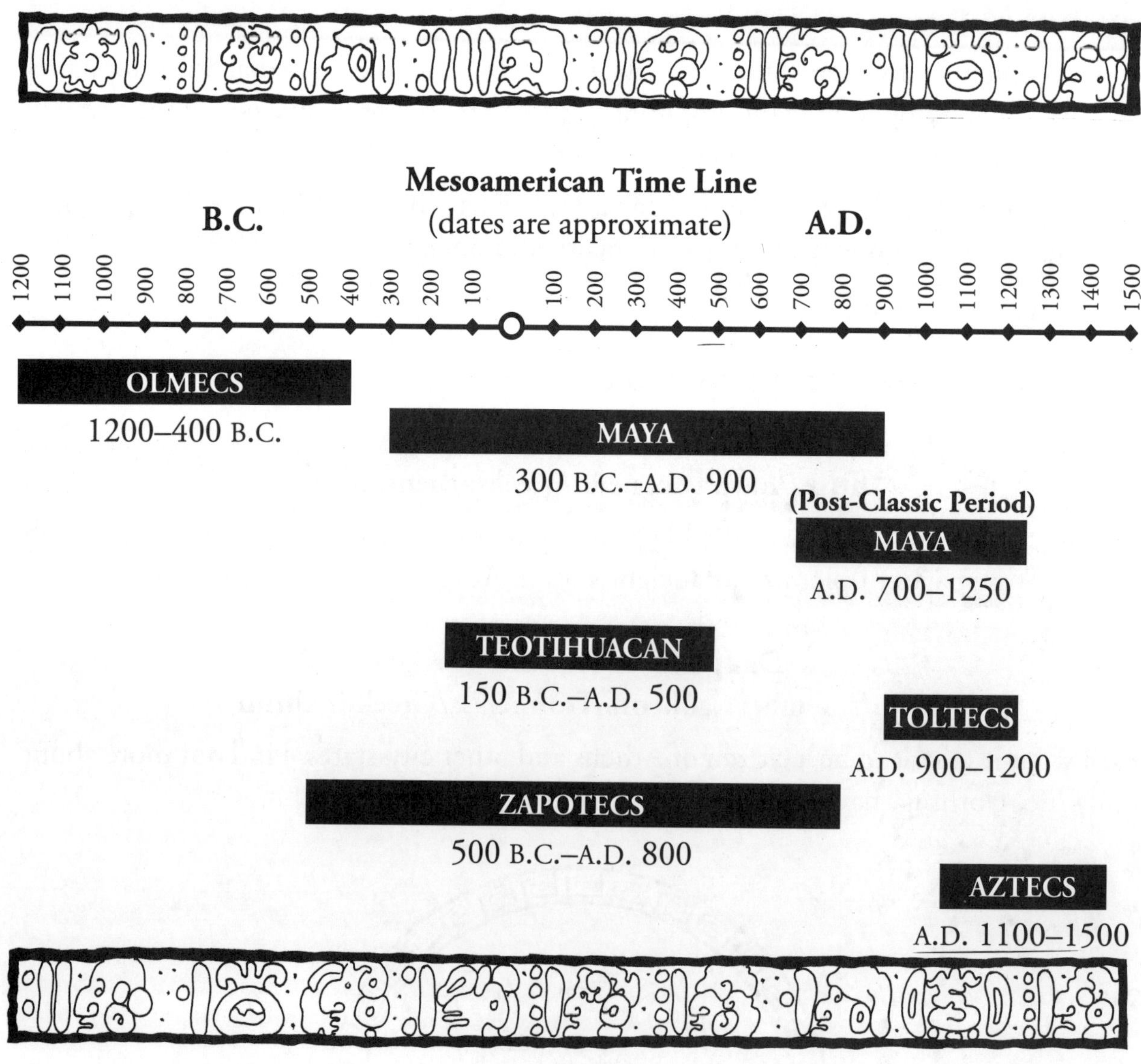

1. After driving about 60 miles (97 km) north of Mexico City, I arrive at the site of the ancient capital of this civilization which dominated much of Mesoamerica. It is the farthest north of any Mesoamerican capital. The archaeological team has just identified a pottery bowl dating from about A.D. 1000. The city itself was the center of a great trading network that reached from the southwestern part of what is now the United States to Costa Rica. It contains several pyramids that have temples built on top of them. One is the temple of Quetzalcóatl, who, according to legend, founded this city. Great columns in the form of serpents and humans support the roof of the temple. Another pyramid-top temple has 15-foot-high (5.5 m) colossal warrior columns reflecting the militant nature of the people. The temple base is adorned with images of jaguars, coyotes, and eagles. "Pacal?" questioned one site worker. "You'll have to travel south to find evidence of him."

   Civilization: ______________________________

   Ancient city: ______________________________

   Modern city and country: ______________________________

2. I drive south to a place about 30 miles (48 km) north of Mexico City. I see a table with some artifacts dated A.D. 200. I learn that this is the site of one of the first major cultures in the Central Valley of Mexico. It was the largest city ever built in ancient Mexico, covering approximately nine square miles (23.3 square km). I walk along the four-mile-long, palace-lined main thoroughfare, called the Street of the Dead. Then I walk around the huge Pyramid of the Sun which is over 200 feet (73 m) high, the Temple of Quetzalcóatl, and the Pyramid of the Moon. The archaeologists smile when I mention Pacal and suggest that I need to drive farther south.

   Civilization: ______________________________

   Ancient city: ______________________________

   Modern country: ______________________________

3. I continue driving farther south to Mexico City where the capital of this civilization was located. It was built on an island and on reclaimed land within a large lake. Three causeways connected the city to the shores. The lake no longer exists, and modern Mexico City is built on top of it. I visit the National Museum of Anthropology and see a mosaic mask from this civilization made of turquoise and dated A.D. 1400, along with other artifacts from the Temple of the War God and the Templo Mayor. The Spanish destroyed all the temples when they conquered these people. I'm still searching for King Pacal, though, and am directed to drive southeast.

   Civilization: ______________________________

   Ancient city: ______________________________

   Modern city and country: ______________________________

4. I drive through the present-day city of Oaxaca to this ancient site atop a ridge. I'm at the location of the civilization's main center. A sign near an archaeological excavation informs me that this city was inhabited from about 500 B.C. to A.D. 800. These people are known for their excellent architecture—temple-pyramids, palaces, richly furnished tombs, an astronomical observatory—and for their ceramic funerary urns with elaborate images of mythological figures. I learn that the oldest evidence of the Mesoamerican calendar came from these people, but I don't see any sign of an ancient king named Pacal. This time I'm heading east.

   Civilization: ______________________________

   Ancient city: ______________________________

   Modern country: ______________________________

5. I'm on a long drive through rain forests and along rivers. I spot all sorts of fruits and flowers, and see many animals including deer, tapir, monkeys, armadillos, and turkeys. I finally make it to the ancient capital of this Mesoamerican civilization, located on the Rio Chiquito about 50 miles (80 km) south of the Tuxtla Mountains. One of the colossal stone heads, a likeness of one of their leaders, is dated at 1200 B.C. It is about 9 feet (3.27 m) tall and weighs about 15 tons (13.6 metric tons). The head is painted a garish purple with dye extracted from a mollusk that lives in the waters off the Gulf Coast. Gigantic basalt slabs decorated with carvings of fantastic animals and humans are located here. These people claimed to be related to jaguars, sacrificed human beings to their gods, and may have taken the heads of conquered foes. But Pacal isn't here, and it is suggested I drive farther east.

   Civilization: ______________________________

   Ancient city: ______________________________

   Modern city and country: ______________________________

6. After an interesting drive, I arrive at what became the second capital of the civilization that erected sculptures of colossal heads. It is located on an island in a swamp near the Tonalá River, about 18 miles (29 km) inland from the Gulf Coast near modern Tabasco. This capital was a civic-ceremonial center. Its political and economic influence spread far beyond the Gulf Coast and reached almost every part of Mesoamerica. The amazing architecture features clay platforms for temples and palaces, and a main pyramid more than 100 feet (36 m) tall. But this is still not the city where Pacal lived, and I am directed even farther east.

   Civilization: ______________________________

   Ancient city: ______________________________

   Modern city and country: ______________________________

7. I realize too late that I've missed the turnoff, so I decide to head up the peninsula to a site that I have heard about. It was the center of its civilization during the Post-Classic Period, located on a dry, semiarid limestone plateau. The people made use of the water in natural sinkholes called *cenotes.* Some of the places I stroll past are the Temple of the Warriors, the very tall pyramid-temple complex called The Castillo, the Great Ball Court (the largest of the many ball courts found at this site), and an astronomical observatory called the Caracol. I also walk down the Sacred Way to the Cenote of Sacrifice and think about the ceremonies that must have taken place here. But other duties await me, so I hurry to my car for the southward journey.

   Civilization: ______________________________

   Ancient city: ______________________________

   Modern region and country: ______________________________

8. I cross the border into the northeast corner of another country and continue south. I arrive at what was the largest city (about 40 square miles or 104 square km) during the period of A.D. 250–900, when there were approximately 75,000 people living there. What amazing buildings—over 3,000 were constructed! I see funerary pyramids, the Great Plaza, reservoirs, and causeways (or roads). I am told to look for Dr. Gonzales at a site farther south.

   Civilization: ______________________________

   Ancient city: ______________________________

   Modern country: ______________________________

9. I enter the northwest corner of another country in Mesoamerica as I continue southward. I want to check out the southernmost city of this civilization. It was a large trading center from about A.D. 250–900 but had been in existence long before that. At least 16 kings ruled in succession and the last king, Yax Pac, had many of the larger buildings constructed. Some of them are the Main Acropolis, a royal palace, a huge and beautiful ball court, and the Hieroglyphic Stairway (a funerary step pyramid whose steps are inscribed with 2,500 glyphs). There are many stelae, but this was not the place where Pacal was king. I'm heading north this time—back into the country where I started this journey.

   Civilization: ______________________________

   Ancient city: ______________________________

   Modern country: ______________________________

10. The drive through Chiapas to this beautiful ancient city is spectacular. I enjoy the sights and sounds of the rain forest—toucans, parrots, macaws, monkeys, and hundreds of insects. I even think I saw a jaguar! Most importantly, I find the elusive Dr. Gonzales, who is so thankful for the information on the stela inscriptions that she gives me a special tour. The highlight is the Temple of the Inscriptions, in which the great Pacal was buried in A.D. 683.

   Civilization: ______________________________

   Ancient city: ______________________________

   Modern state and country: ______________________________

Discover More

- Much of what we know about ancient civilizations is based on what archaeologists find and how they interpret their findings. Imagine that a future archaeologist at an excavation site uncovers the remains of a store selling Halloween candy, costumes, and decorations. How do you think the archaeologist might interpret his or her findings? In your answer, consider holiday ceremonies or rituals, special clothing and objects used in the ceremony, the people who participated, and the purpose of the event.
- For many of the Mesoamerican civilizations, chocolate was a highly-valued food. Usually it was the drink of the wealthy. Cacao beans were so prized that they were used as money. Which foods in our culture are so highly valued that they are given as gifts?

Learn More on the Internet

Pre-Columbian Culture
http://udgftp.cencar.udg.mx/ingles/Precolombina/precointro.html

Written and maintained by the University of Guadalajara, this Web site has sections on the Aztecs (the Mexicas), the Maya, and the Olmecs.

Major Indian Influences in Latin America
http://www2.localaccess.com/chappell/latin_america/indians.htm

Created by Dave Chappell, a Spanish instructor at W. F. West High School in Chehalis, Washington, this Web site has excellent sections with pictures, text, and maps on the Inca, Maya, Toltec, and Aztec civilizations.

Ice Mummies of the Inca
http://www.pbs.org/wgbh/nova/peru/

Join a NOVA team on an expedition to Peru. Fascinating information is found by clicking on "The Expedition," "Mummies," "Lost Worlds," "Newsflash," and "Resources." To read questions written by others, or to ask your own question, click on "Mail."

Try these Web sites on the Maya:

Information on the Ancient Maya Civilization
http://pacific.st.usm.edu/~tgparker/maya.html

The Maya Astronomy Page
http://www.astro.uva.nl/michielb/maya/astro.html

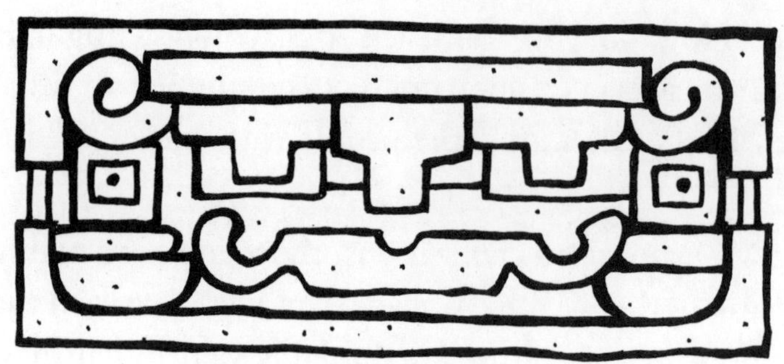

The Stolen Jade Necklace

Dragon Lee, the notorious thief wanted in all corners of China, has stolen an exotic jade necklace from the Peaceful Summer Palace in Beijing. The palace staff has hired Detective Lin, private investigator, and has given her the responsibility of finding and arresting Dragon Lee, and returning the jade necklace to the Empress. It will be an overwhelming task. Dragon Lee is sure to be hiding in one of the places important to the ancient civilization of China, because she has a special fondness for history and antiquities. China is a huge country, so Lin is anxious to start the search. You're welcome to come along with her, but she won't tell you where you are. On your journey, you'll get to enjoy amazing sights and test your knowledge of ancient China.

1. Lin's first stop is the best known place in all of China. It is a 47-mile (96 km) trip from Beijing to a spot called Badaling. Lin sees thousands of people climbing all over the structure and walking along the top, 25 feet (8 m) high, where warriors and horses used to gallop 10 abreast. The building of this structure began in the 400s B.C. for protection from nomadic tribes. It would eventually become the longest structure ever built, stretching for nearly 4,000 miles (6,440 km). Lin spends most of the afternoon here, but she doesn't spot Dragon Lee.

2. Lin drives south of Beijing, heading to a place outside of Shanghai called Hangzhou. This is the southern beginning of this man-made waterway that extends 1,000 miles (1,610 km) to near Beijing in the north. It was begun in the fourth century B.C. and completed in the A.D. 1200s. The waterway, while still a major link uniting the north and south, is not as important today as the railways. Lin hires a junk and looks for several days to see if Dragon Lee has made her way here. But Dragon Lee is nowhere in sight.

3. It isn't an easy drive, but Lin arrives in another of China's bustling cities, a major industrial center located in Shaanxi province along the Wei River. It was the capital of ancient China for more than 1,000 years; its name at that time was Chang'an. It is surrounded by a wall dating from the Ming Dynasty that has towers, arched gateways, and large red-roofed sentry posts. It was a main stopping place for Silk Road traders. This is an important stop for Lin because several short side trips can be made from here. While she's here, she will investigate the markets, parks, and major shopping centers looking for Dragon Lee.

4. Just a few miles east of Lin's hotel, in the ancient capital, is an even older site. Scientists think this was where people gave up migratory hunting and became farmers. It is one of the spots known as a birthplace of Chinese culture. Lin visits an excavated village from the Yang-shao culture (c. 3000 B.C.) where people lived in close-knit family groups and joined together to form tribes. They planted crops, irrigated fields, and tended animals. They are famous for their clay coil pots which were painted with what are thought to be the forerunners of modern Chinese characters. Lin searches the museum and excavation site and inquires about Dragon Lee, but no one has seen her. (Hint: the name of the village starts with the letter "B.")

5. It's back to the hotel for a rest and then another short drive to an amazing burial complex in the hills near Lin's hotel. Nearly 700,000 workers spent 36 years building 6,000 life-sized, terra-cotta warrior statues to guard the tomb of the first emperor of China. Each statue wore the uniform of his rank. There were officers, cavalrymen with horses, and charioteers. This unbelievable army of clay soldiers was placed 15 feet (5.45 m) underground, and a wooden roof was built over them which was covered with soil. These soldiers were found in 1973, and in 1990 another find was made—thousands of terra-cotta sculptures of men, boys, horses, and carts. Lin mingles with the tourists, but Lee hasn't come here.

6. Lin continues to south China and the Guangxi region to a picturesque city that was founded in the third century at the time of the construction of the Lingzhu Canal. It is located on the Li River and has scenery that has inspired poets and artists for centuries—limestone hills eroded into peaks, caves, rice paddies, a mist rising from the river where water buffalo eat, and fishermen and farmers slowly going about their daily chores. Lin takes several trips along the Li River but without luck; none of the boat navigators has seen Dragon Lee.

7. Lin is now in Sichuan province heading for a city along the Min River which is south of Chengdu. The tourist attraction here is a colossal Buddha; its middle fingers alone are 27 feet (8.2 m) long. It is the largest of its kind in China, measuring 233 feet (71 m) in height. The sculpted Buddha was started in A.D. 713 and took 90 years to complete. It is carved into the cliffs which tower above the confluence of three rivers. Tradition has it that the figure was created in the hope that it would encourage the Buddha himself to calm the turbulent waters in this spot where many had met death by drowning. Walking down from the gigantic Buddha, Lin asks a group of tourists if they have seen Dragon Lee. They have heard rumors that she likes to hide out in Tibet. (Hint: the name of the city begins with the letter "L.")

8. Lin has to leave her car overnight at the airport and fly into Tibet, as driving over the Himalayas would prove a daunting task. She goes to the capital of Tibet, 12,002 feet (3,658 m) above sea level. The capital is the religious center of Tibetan Buddhism and was settled as early as the fifth century. It is the traditional home of the Dalai Lama, the head of the Tibetan Buddhists. Unfortunately, the trip to Tibet looks like a wild goose chase for Lin.

9. Back at the airport in Chengdu, Lin decides to try another theory. She flies to an isolated city in northwest China, the capital of the autonomous region of Xinjiang. Here tourists can see how the Uigurs live. They sleep in *yurts*, comfortable homes that are circular felt tents about 24 feet (7.3 m) in diameter. They eat traditional meals consisting of mutton, cheese, and fermented mare's milk, and they enjoy equestrian shows and shooting competitions. This city was also one of the oasis stops for caravans on the Silk Road. One of the Uigurs pulls Lin aside and says a woman tried to sell him a jade necklace. Could it be Dragon Lee? The man heard she was headed for the capital.

10. Lin is in the modern capital now, a place that was occupied by Peking Man about 500,000 years ago. She walks around Tiananmen Square, one of the largest square plazas in the world, trying to spot Dragon Lee. She tours the Great Hall of the People, and then heads for the Gate of Heavenly Peace, the entrance to the Forbidden City. The Forbidden City served as court for 24 emperors over a period of five centuries. There, in one of the hundreds of ancient palaces, she spots Dragon Lee. Before long she has her in custody and has the jade necklace safely in her backpack. On the way to the Celestial Prison, Dragon Lee promises she will reform and will never steal again.

Can you identify the places Detective Lin stopped? Write their names on the lines below.

1. ______________________ 6. ______________________

2. ______________________ 7. ______________________

3. ______________________ 8. ______________________

4. ______________________ 9. ______________________

5. ______________________ 10. ______________________

Discover More

- Find a map of China in an atlas and trace the route that Detective Lin took to find Dragon Lee. Choose the place where you would most like to do some sightseeing. Explain why you would like to visit this spot.
- Another historical site is the Valley of the Ming Tombs where 13 Ming emperors are buried. It is just north of Beijing. Inside most of the tombs are breathtaking objects—tiaras covered in pearls, priceless vases, carved statuettes, and silk robes. Design your own tomb for a famous Chinese ruler. Make it unique and beautiful, and furnish it with objects befitting royalty.

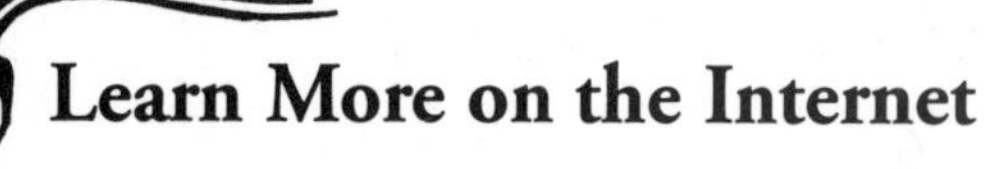

Learn More on the Internet

Empires Beyond the Great Wall, The Heritage of Genghis Khan
http://www.dataflux.bc.ca/khan/index.html

View treasures and ancient artifacts from the steppes of Inner Mongolia as you tour the exhibit at the Royal British Columbia Museum. Click on "The Culture," "The Artifacts," "Genghis Khan," and "Exhibit Info."

CG World—The Ancient World Revisited
http://www.taisei.co.jp/cg_e/cg.html

This Web page is produced by Taisei Corporation in Japan. Click on "The Ancient World Revisited" to access beautiful images of ancient civilizations. For China, try "Dadu (Beijing)," "Shi huangdil ing," and "Karatorum." You can also see images from Mesoamerica, Egypt, the Aztec Empire, and Rome.

China the Beautiful
http://chinapage.com/china-rm.html

Listen to sounds of Chinese, explore the art of calligraphy, view paintings, read poetry, learn about dragons, and discover more about ancient Chinese history.

The Development of Western Civilization: China
http://history.evansville.net/china.html

This Web site contains links to many sites on the topics of Chinese history, art, architecture, literature, music, dance, and daily life.

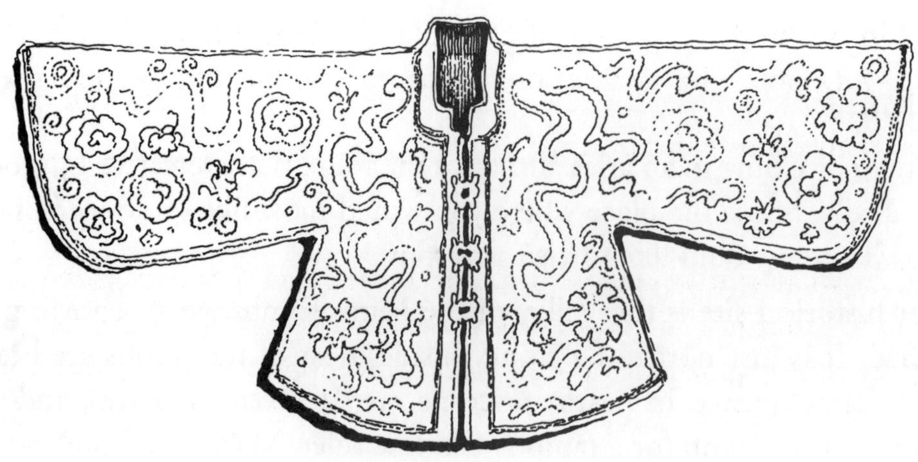

A Tour of Kush and Axum

We are just about ready to board our jeeps to begin a trip through places important to the ancient kingdoms of Kush and Axum. Kush and Axum aren't as well known as their neighbor to the north, Egypt, but they were influential trading and cultural centers.

See if you can identify some of the important places and things we will be seeing and learning about on our trip.

1. Located in the modern country of Ethiopia, this kingdom reached its height from 500 B.C.–A.D. 600. This civilization was strongly influenced by Arabia and Greece.

   Can you name this civilization? ____________________

2. Located in what is now southern Egypt and northern Sudan, this was the most important civilization in the region known as Nubia. It was a major civilization during the time period of 2000 B.C.–A.D. 400. Egyptian wall paintings show the people as black Africans.

   Can you name this civilization? ____________________

3. The kingdom of Kush was mostly desert, but life in this civilization was nourished by the river which ran through it. This great river is the same one that supplied water and fertile soil to the Egyptians north of Kush. Two branches of this river converge at this city.

   Can you name the city and the two branches of the river? ____________________

   ____

4. Kush's first capital was located just below the fourth ***cataract*** on the river. This was the heart of the Kush kingdom. It is also near this capital that Kushite kings first built pyramids similar to those seen in Egypt. They were slightly smaller, and the mummies were placed under rather than inside the pyramids.

   Can you name the first capital of Kush? ______________________________

5. Around 750 B.C., the Kushite army defeated the strong nation to its north and the Kushite rulers founded the 25th Dynasty. They established their capital at Memphis. Their rule of this country lasted less than 100 years, and ended when the country was conquered by the Assyrians. The Kushite rulers returned to their own capital. One of the most important Kushite kings of the 25th Dynasty was this king who ruled from 690–664 B.C. He is even mentioned in the Bible as "Tirhaka." He built his pyramid at Nuri in Kush, which was probably inspired by the pyramids at Giza.

   Can you name the country where pharaohs ruled? ______________________

   Can you name the great Kush pharaoh? ______________________________

6. The Assyrian army destroyed the first capital of Kush, so the Kushites moved their capital to another city. It became a great cultural and trading center and was the center of iron making because of the vast deposits of iron ore found nearby. It may also have been from this location that iron-casting techniques spread through ancient Africa. Now the Kushites were free from influences from the north and were able to develop new styles in art and architecture, invent their own system of writing, and build royal palaces, temples, and a group of pyramids.

   Can you name the Kushites' new capital? ______________________________

7. Ramses II of Egypt built several major temples in Kushite territory. He wanted to emphasize that Kush was under his control. Two of the most famous temples are dedicated to him and to his queen, Nefertari. Four huge statues stand in front of these famous temples, which are known collectively as the Great Temple. When work began on the Aswan Dam in the 1960s, the temple site was covered by the waters of Lake Nasser, but the temple itself was moved to a man-made cliff above water level.

   Can you name the location of Ramses' Great Temple? ____________________

8. The most important port city of Axum was a main stopping place for traders and merchants. They brought cargoes of frankincense, myrrh, spices, gold, lacquerware, and pet monkeys. Ivory from the interior of Africa was shipped to Arabia, India, and the Mediterranean. This bustling port city was near what is now Massawa.

   Can you name this ancient port city? ________________________________

9. The capital of Axum was a powerful trading city. Many palaces and granite monuments were built in and around the city. It is located in the northwest corner of the province of Tigre in northern Ethiopia. Its name is similar to "Axum."

   Can you name the capital of Axum? ____________________

10. During the A.D. 300s, skilled Axumite stonemasons erected hundreds of huge granite monuments as a sign of their country's wealth and power. These tall, narrow monuments were carved to resemble multistoried buildings. Some are carved with symbols of gods. One of the largest ones is still standing; it measures about 98 feet (30 m) in height and it has started to lean.

    Can you name these tall, narrow monuments? ____________________

Discover More

- Do research to find out more about these Kush kings who ruled in Egypt: Kashta, Piankhy (Piye), Shabaka, and Taharqa (Tirhaka).
- The Kushite pharaohs wore the double crown of the Egyptian pharaohs, but some wore a crown with two sacred cobras. Design a unique crown which contains a cobra, the rays of the sun, and a falcon. Label each part and explain its significance.

Learn More on the Internet

Civilizations in Africa: Axum
http://www.wsu.edu:8080/~dee/CIVAFRCA/AXUM.HTM

This Web site was created by Richard Hooker of Washington State University.

The Gateway of Nubia
http://uts.cc.utexas.edu/~rocman/index.htm

Be sure to click on the "Picture Gallery" at the end of the page.

National Museum of African Art
http://www.si.edu/organiza/museums/africart/exhibits/currexhb.htm

The museum's exhibits change, but on long-term loan is "The Ancient Nubian City of Kerma, 2500–1500 B.C.," which features 40 objects.

The Seven Wonders of the Ancient World

Welcome to Ancient World Investigations. We are happy to have so many mystery buffs with us at this conference. We invited you because we need your help to solve a perplexing problem. As you know, a list exists of what are considered to be the Seven Wonders of the Ancient World. One of the first references to the Seven Wonders is found in the ancient Greek historian Herodotus' *History*. The Seven Wonders are mentioned in other ancient books, as well. Scientists are still uncovering information about the Seven Wonders, trying to prove their existence, and learning more about their importance.

Last year we were given a mysterious-looking, leather-bound case containing 14 handwritten descriptions of amazing places, and 7 charcoal sketches of buildings and monuments. The problem is that we are having difficulty matching the descriptions to the sketches. Do you think you can help us? Let's get to work!

Description 1: The trek through the desert did not prepare us for the vision ahead. We are staring at what must be the tallest structure on Earth! It is covered with stones to smooth its surface and the whole structure must consist of more than two million blocks of stone, each weighing several tons. On the north face is the entrance which leads to a number of corridors, galleries, and escape shafts. In the heart of the structure is the king's chamber where he will be buried.

Description 2: As we approach this structure, we cannot believe our eyes. We are sure that nowhere else in the world could there be a man-made structure like this. It is a series of terraces rising into the sky. On the terraces are palm trees, fruit trees, flowering plants, exotic animals, streams, and waterfalls. The spectacular city of Nebuchadnezzar is a wonder to behold.

Description 3: As we climb the hill near where the Olympic Games are held, our destination is the magnificent temple built to honor the "king of the gods." It attracts visitors and worshippers from all over the world, but many of them come to view what is inside the temple—definitely a wonder of the world. It is a sculpture of a figure by Pheidias, who began work around 440 B.C. Parts of it are made from ivory, and the sandals and robe are made from gold. Our eyes travel upward 40 feet (12 m) to the very top and discover that it barely clears the ceiling.

Description 4: It is said that the sun itself has never looked upon this building's equal. This beautiful structure is made of marble, with a decorated façade overlooking a large courtyard. Marble steps surround the building platform and lead to the high terrace; 127 columns cover the platform area. Dedicated to the goddess whom the Romans call Diana, this building is a wonder to behold.

Description 5: This structure staggers the imagination. From our vantage point atop our camels, it looks like a mountain rising out of the desert. There are two other similar structures nearby but they are neither as large nor as old. Off to one side is a large stone sculpture in the shape of the mythological sphinx—a lion with a man's head.

Description 6: We've found a tomb adorned with statues of horses and men realistically carved from marble of the best quality—its beauty alone makes this a wonder of the ancient world. It is the burial place of King Mausolus of Caria who reigned from 377–353 B.C. in a region of ancient Persia. Its location is known today as Bodrum, on the coast of the Aegean Sea.

Description 7: At the time this marvel was built, Greece was comprised of city-states. This wonder is located on an island of three city-states: Ialysos, Kamiros, and Lindos. In 408 B.C., the cities united to form one territory and erected this enormous monument to their sun god, Helios, in celebration of unification.

Description 8: This 23-foot (7 m) tall structure is situated by the Euphrates River in order to take advantage of the water, which is used to irrigate the plants growing on its high terraces. We hear that the king's wife missed the mountains of her native Persia, so the king built this stacked-terraced structure to make her feel more at home.

Description 9: Not only are we amazed by the beautiful tomb itself, but the ornamentation on the inside is breathtaking, as well. There are decorations and statues adorning the outside at different levels on the podium and the roof. There are numerous life-sized statues of people, lions, horses, and other animals; some of the statues are larger than life-size! The sarcophagus, of white alabaster decorated with gold, is surrounded by columns. On the very top of the tomb is a chariot pulled by four horses. The Persian king has one of the most beautiful tombs in the world.

Description 10: This throne has carvings of sphinxes, winged figures of Victory, gods, and mythical figures. It is decorated with gold, precious stones, ebony, and ivory. The statue's head is adorned with a wreath of olive sprays, and its left hand holds a scepter with an eagle perched on top. Its robe is carved with animals and lilies. We are inside a temple that fell into ruins after the Olympic Games were banned in A.D. 391.

Description 11: In addition to being a religious institution, this structure served as a marketplace. Merchants, tourists, artisans, and royalty paid homage to the goddess of the hunt and moon, bringing earrings, necklaces, and statuettes as offerings. Inside are many works of art including paintings, four ancient bronze statues of Amazons, golden pillars, and silver statuettes. The ancient city which contained this structure is near the modern town of Selcuk in Turkey.

Description 12: On the ancient island of Pharos, we stand in awe of one of the tallest structures on Earth. This monument helped ships navigate in dangerous sailing conditions and ensured them a safe return to one of the great harbors of the world. A statue of Poseidon adorns the summit of this building.

Description 13: This colossal monument was erected on the eastern promontory of the Mandraki harbor (not at the harbor entrance as was once believed). With a base of white marble, the monument stands about 110 feet (33.5 m) high. It is so big that no one in our group is able to make their arms meet around its thumb. The sculptor of the Statue of Liberty was inspired by this wonder of the world.

Description 14: This structure is located near the city named for Alexander the Great. The total height of the building is about 384 feet (117 m), equivalent to a 40-story modern building. The internal core is a shaft used to lift fuel to light the fire that guided ships at night. At the top stage, a mirror reflects sunlight during the day. Some say the mirror was used to detect and burn enemy ships before they could reach the shore.

The Seven Charcoal Sketches

Can you match each description to one of the Seven Wonders of the World? Each wonder will be used twice. As an added challenge, include the name of the civilization where each "wonder" is (or was) found.

1. ______________________________

____

2. ______________________________

____

3. ______________________________

____

4. ______________________________

____

5. ______________________________

____

6. ______________________________

____

7. ______________________________

____

8. ______________________________

____

9. ______________________________

____

10. ______________________________

____

11. ____

____

12. ____

____

13. ____

____

14. ____

____

Discover More

- Locate each of the Ancient Wonders on a map. Then pretend that you are an adventurer who travels to exotic places. Create a diary entry in which you record your experiences during a day trip to visit one of the Ancient Wonders.
- Make a list of the Seven Wonders of the Modern World, the Seven Wonders of North and South America, and the Seven Imaginary Wonders of the Universe.

Learn More on the Internet

The Seven Wonders of the Ancient World
http://pharos.bu.edu/Egypt/Wonders/

This site contains pictures, information, and detailed descriptions of each of the Seven Wonders of the Ancient World.

Glossary

A.D. an abbreviation for the Latin phrase, *anno Domini,* literally meaning "in the year of our Lord"

agora the marketplace or open meeting place of ancient Greece

ambrosia the food of the Greek and Roman gods; a dessert made of oranges and shredded coconut

anthropologist a person who studies the science of the origins and development of human societies and the differences between them

ascetic a person who practices self-denial. In ancient Greece, asceticism referred to the discipline practiced by athletes; in early religious groups, it meant extreme self-denial and fasting to gain spiritual strength.

B.C. an abbreviation for the phrase "before Christ"

basilica an oblong building of ancient Rome or Greece having two rows of columns dividing the interior into a nave and two side aisles. A basilica was used as a court or place of assembly. The pope of the Roman Catholic Church can designate certain churches and cathedrals "basilicas."

caldarium a pool of hot water in a Roman bath

canopic jar ancient Egyptian containers which held the organs of a person being mummified

cataract a waterfall, especially a large one over a precipice, or steep rapids in a river

chiton the basic clothing of ancient Greeks, worn knee-length by men and full-length by women

circa means "about" and is used before approximate dates or figures

colonnades a series of columns set at regular intervals and usually supporting the base of a roof structure

comitium meeting place in ancient Rome

curia the place of assembly of certain ruling groups in ancient Rome

damask a rich, patterned fabric first woven in silk, and named for Damascus, Syria

Doric the oldest and simplest of the three orders of classical Greek architecture, characterized by thick and powerful columns with no base and a plain, round capital

Glossary
(continued)

frieze a sculptured or richly ornamented band along the upper part of a Greek building between the tops of the columns and the roofline

frigidarium a pool of cold water in a Roman bath

glyph a symbol or figure in the Maya language which stands for a number, name, or word

hydrias a Greek vessel used to hold and carry water

indigenous people, ideas, or plants that originate, or occur naturally, in a particular region or environment

Ionic an order of Greek architecture distinguished by fluted columns on rounded bases and spiral scroll-like capitals

junk a type of Chinese ship with a high poop, batten sails, little or no keel, and high pole masts

karma one's accumulated good and bad deeds in previous existences; a religious term in Buddhism and Hinduism

krater a Greek jar or vase having a large round body and a wide mouth; used for mixing wine and water

linear referring to an ancient form of writing used in Crete called Linear A

mastaba an ancient Egyptian tomb that is oblong in shape with sloping sides and a flat roof

reincarnation to be reborn in another body

rostrum a dais or platform used for public speaking in ancient Rome

skene the dressing rooms behind the stage at an ancient Greek theater

tepidarium a pool of warm water in a Roman bath

thermae a Roman bath

yang the masculine part of nature in Chinese cosmology characterized by light, heat, or dryness

yin the feminine part of nature in Chinese cosmology characterized by darkness, cold, or wetness

ziggurat a huge temple tower with the form of a terraced pyramid popular in Mesopotamia

Answer Key

The Fertile Crescent Puzzle
Pages 8–14

1. the ziggurat of Ur; Ur
2. Hanging Gardens; Babylon
3. bull's head; Çatalhöyük (Çatal Hüyük)
4. bulla; Sumer
5. personal seal; Sumer
6. Ishtar Gate; Babylon
7. Code of Hammurabi; Babylon
8. mud bricks; Jericho
9. Epic of Gilgamesh; Uruk
10. wheel; Sumer

A River Runs Through It
Pages 15–18

1. Indus River
2. Tigris River
3. Euphrates River
4. Tiber River
5. Jordan River
6. Nile River
7. Ganges River
8. Huang He or Ho (or Yellow River)
9. Yangtze River
10. Usumacinta River

The Mysterious Silk Road
Pages 19–22

1. Byzantium or Constantinople
2. Tyre
3. Damascus
4. Baghdad
5. Samarkand
6. Tashkent
7. Pamirs Mountains
8. Kashgar
9. Taklamakan Desert
10. Xi'an (Chang'an)

Answer Key
(continued)

Fib or Truth?
Pages 23–26

1. Hammurabi
2. Imhotep
3. Cheops/Khufu
4. Chandragupta Maurya
5. David
6. Qin Shihuang
7. Hannibal
8. Plato
9. Julius Caesar
10. Confucius
11. #3: Giza not Abel Simbel; "Great Pyramid" not "Amazing Pyramid"
12. #7: elephants, not camels

Ancient Religion Mix-Up
Pages 27–31

1. Hinduism
2. Daoism
3. Christianity
4. Judaism
5. (blank)
6. Confucianism
7. Islam
8. Shinto
9. Jainism
10. Buddhism
11. Çatalhöyük

Clues to Ancient Writing
Pages 32–36

1. cuneiform; Sumerian
2. Indus Valley seals; Indus Valley
3. writing on oracle bones; China
4. an alphabet; Phoenicians
5. hieroglyphic writing; Maya
6. hieroglyphs; Egypt
7. Linear A; Crete or Minoan
8. Latin; Rome
9. the futhark or runic alphabet; Vikings
10. Greek; Greece

Answer Key
(continued)

Architectural Wonders
Pages 37–40

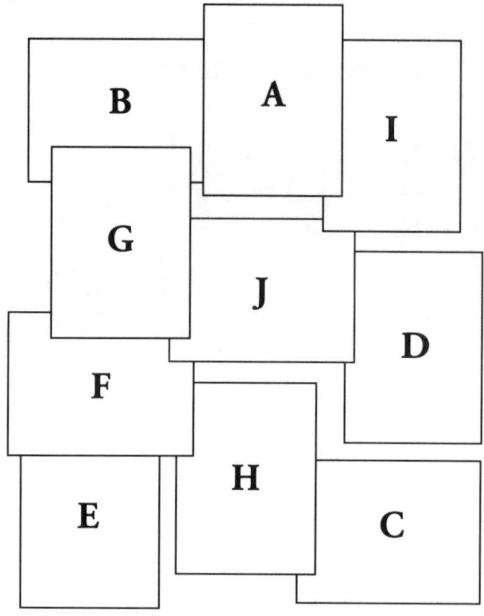

Literary Scavenger Hunt
Pages 41–45

1. Book of Kells; Ireland
2. Book of the Dead; Egypt
3. Dead Sea Scrolls; Israel, Jerusalem
4. the Torah; Israel
5. Tale of Gilgamesh; Sumer or Mesopotamia
6. the Vedas; India
7. Aesop's Fables/Aesop; Greece
8. Sophocles; Greece
9. Lao Tzu (Laozi); China
10. Iliad and Odyssey; Greece

An Ancient Artifact
Pages 46–50

1. Sumerians; Iraq
2. Babylonians; Iraq
3. Hittites; Turkey
4. Phoenicians; Lebanon
5. Minoans; Crete
6. Myceneans; Greece
7. Etruscans; Italy
8. Celts; Ireland
9. Inca; Peru
10. Maya; Guatemala, Mexico

Answer Key
(continued)

Invention Selection
Pages 51–54

1. irrigation; Sumer in Mesopotamia
2. ink; Egypt
3. plow; Sumer in Mesopotamia
4. medical instruments; Babylon
5. alphabet; Phoenicia
6. bells; China
7. aqueduct; Assyria
8. pontoon bridge; Persia
9. Archimedes' screw; Egypt
10. paper; China
11. chess; India
12. gunpowder; China

Be Aware of Angry Gods!
Pages 56–59

1. Zeus
2. Poseidon
3. Athena
4. Apollo
5. Aphrodite
6. Ares
7. Hera
8. Hephaestus
9. Hestia
10. Hermes
11. Hades
12. Artemis

The Mystery of the Stolen Shards
Pages 60–64

A. Athens
B. Marathon
C. Olympus
D. Sparta
E. Ithaca
F. Delphi
G. Argos
H. Mycenae
I. Andros
J. Corinth

Answer Key
(continued)

Let's Play *Q&A!*
Pages 71–75

1. Who are Remus and Romulus?
2. Who is Julius Caesar?
3. Who is Octavian (Augustus Caesar)?
4. What are the Roman baths?
5. What is the Roman forum?
6. Who are Jupiter, Diana, and Neptune?
7. Who is Constantine I (Constantine the Great)?
8. What is the Colosseum?
9. What is the Via Appia Antica (or the Appian Way)?
10. What is Pompeii?

Search Along the Nile
Pages 65–70

1. Alexandria
2. Giza
3. Saqqara
4. Memphis
5. Tell el-Amarna (Amarna)
6. Dendera
7. Karnak
8. Valley of the Kings
9. Edfu
10. Abu Simbel

Answer Key
(continued)

Lost in Ancient Athens
Pages 76–79

1. agora
2. gymnasium
3. theater
4. Panathenaic Way
5. Acropolis
6. Propylaeum
7. Temple of Athena Nike
8. Statue of Athena
9. Parthenon
10. Erechtheion

The Stolen Jade Necklace
Pages 87–92

1. Great Wall of China
2. Grand Canal
3. Xi'an
4. village of Ban-po
5. terra-cotta warriors
6. Guilin
7. Leshan
8. Lhasa
9. Ürümqi
10. Beijing

Adventures in Mesoamerica
Pages 80–86

1. Toltecs; Tollan (Tula in Spanish); Hidalgo, Mexico
2. Teotihuacan; Teotihuacan; Mexico
3. Aztecs; Tenochtitlán; Mexico City, Mexico
4. Zapotecs; Monte Albán; Mexico
5. Olmecs; San Lorenzo; Veracruz, Mexico
6. Olmecs; La Venta; Veracruz, Mexico
7. Maya; Chitchén Itzá; Yucatan, Mexico
8. Maya; Tikal; Guatemala
9. Maya; Copán; Honduras
10. Maya; Palenque; Chiapas State, Mexico

Answer Key
(continued)

A Tour of Kush and Axum
Pages 93–97

1. Axum
2. Kush
3. Khartoum; the Blue and White Nile
4. Napata
5. Egypt; Taharqa
6. Meroë
7. Abu Simbel
8. Adulis
9. Aksum
10. obelisks or stelae

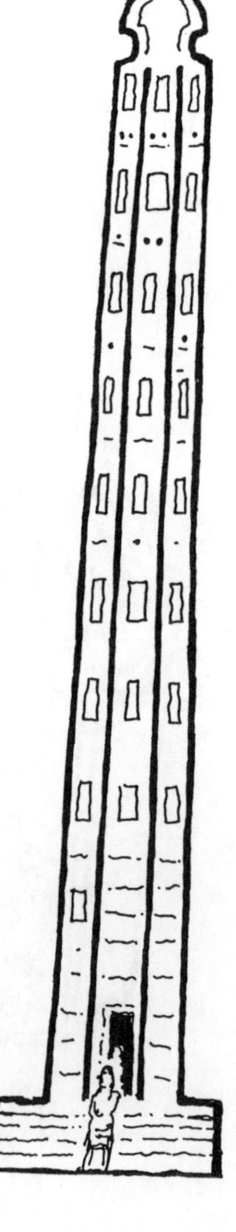

The Seven Wonders of the Ancient World
Pages 98–103

1. the Great Pyramid; Egypt
2. the Hanging Gardens of Babylon; Babylon
3. the statue of Zeus at Olympia; Greece (Olympia)
4. the temple of Artemis at Ephesus; Greece (Ephesus)
5. the Great Pyramid; Egypt
6. the Mausoleum at Halicarnassus; present-day Turkey (Halicarnassus, known today as Bodrum)
7. the Colossus of Rhodes; Rhodes, Greece
8. the Hanging Gardens of Babylon; Babylon
9. the Mausoleum at Halicarnassus; present-day Turkey (Halicarnassus, known today as Bodrum)
10. the statue of Zeus at Olympia; Greece (Olympia)
11. the temple of Artemis at Ephesus; Greece (Ephesus)
12. the Lighthouse of Alexandria (sometimes called the Pharos of Alexandria); Alexandria, Egypt
13. the Colossus of Rhodes; Rhodes, Greece
14. the Lighthouse of Alexandria (sometimes called the Pharos of Alexandria); Alexandria, Egypt